THE
INLAND RESORTS
AND SPAS OF
BRITAIN

THE INLAND RESORTS AND SPAS OF BRITAIN

Frederick Alderson

DAVID & CHARLES: NEWTON ABBOT

0 7153 6048 5

Set in 11/13 Bembo
and printed in Great Britain
by Butler & Tanner Frome and London
for David & Charles (Holdings) Limited
South Devon House Newton Abbot Devon

CONTENTS

		Page
	Introduction	9
1	Early Watering Places	16
2	Fashion-Setters	23
3	Eighteenth-Century Imitators	44
4	Regency Rivals	59
5	Victorian Developments	73
6	Spa-lets	96
7	Wells in Wales	112
8	Picturesque Resorts	120
9	Heath and Forest Centres	139
10	Inland Resorts Today: A Gazetteer	148
	Select Bibliography	184
	Index	187

LIST OF ILLUSTRATIONS

PLATES

	Page
The Pantiles, Tunbridge Wells (*S. K. Lazell*)	33
Royal Crescent, Bath (*Bath City Council*)	33
Bath Abbey, Abbey churchyard and Pump Room (*Bath City Council*)	34
Bath	51
Matlock Bath	51
Municipal offices, Cheltenham (*Cheltenham Corporation*)	52
Cheltenham's classic Promenade (*Cheltenham Corporation*)	52
Malvern Priory and Abbey Hotel	85
The Kursaal, Harrogate	85
The Winter Gardens, Harrogate	86
Spa Well, Low Harrogate, in 1829 (*English Life Publications, Derby*)	103
The John Well, Harrogate, in 1796 (*English Life Publications, Derby*)	103
Dinsdale Spa, Durham	104
Gilsland Spa, Cumberland	104

IN TEXT

	Page
Map	14
Buxton	46
Leamington	60
Cheltenham	66
Ben Rhydding	82

	Page
Troutbeck Hydropathic Establishment, Ilkley	83
Advertisement for carriages, Ilkley	88
Dorton Chalybeate (title page)	106
The Pump, Shap Spa	110
Bowness	123
Winandermere	125
Advertisement for boarding house	126
Advertisement for Bowness hotel	128
Windermere	131
Lyndhurst	141
Bridge of Allan	143
Ochil Mountains	146

INTRODUCTION

'Cathedral cities, regional capitals and health resorts are the English towns which by tradition and convention may be visited for the pure pleasure of visiting them.'

SIR JOHN SUMMERSON

BRITAIN IS fortunate in having, well spread across her counties, a good number of towns that have been developed with a style and for a purpose other than that of industry, trade or commerce. One considerable group of them, comprising some of the most attractive and individual types of British town, is formed by the health-and-pleasure resorts. These often, though not always, antedate the coastal health resorts and, by reason of their greater variety of situation and region, have more distinctive personalities than are found in the general run of seaside towns, while at the same time usually sharing recognisable features.

Most of those resort towns that have been purpose built, like Leamington, Buxton, Harrogate, Bath, have on their common features the impress of assured architectural periods. And, more than most towns, they have so far managed to keep their original face and character reasonably intact, even if the body itself has acquired different proportions. Those which were not, in origin, purpose built as resorts, like Droitwich, Dolgelley, Ambleside, have subscribed to the policy of preserving a later resort image. The same applies, in general, though with rather less architectural emphasis, to inland resorts in Scotland. They are nearly all towns well worth visiting for their own sake. If they were to adopt a common motto, it would be, presumably, OTIUM CUM DIGNITATE.

9

'After the play I came home, ate a Bath cake and a sweet orange, and went comfortably to bed.' Had everybody of Boswell's day (he was diary-writing in 1763) and of the generation or two before and after it, supped, or dined, as frugally, it is doubtful whether the spa resort would have enjoyed its extraordinary rise to popularity in that period. Gout and other rheumatic ailments which afflicted the seventeenth- and eighteenth-century aristocracy so persistently were largely due to excessive port and sherry drinking; an almost exclusively meat and wheat diet produced further afflictions. In the Middle Ages, when food was scarce and over-eating singular and conspicuous, gluttony had been denounced as a sin. Now, when it was commonplace, it had to be dealt with by therapy. The water cure seemed to be the answer: both empirical observation and scientific disquisition (such as 'A discourse of natural bathes and minerall waters' by Edward Jorden, 1631) supported it. For the rich and aristocratic cure-seekers a succession of routs, balls, assemblies, facilities for gambling at cards or dice, were the de rigueur accompaniments to a course of treatment. The need for public rooms and suitable private accommodation thus gave to developers and speculators, men of enterprise, landowners allied with architects of distinction, the opportunity to create new towns on a new pattern, with the layout of Bath as early exemplar.

An important contributor to both the growth and the appearance of these towns was the greater ease of travel and greater volume of traffic of the roads, made possible during the eighteenth and early nineteenth centuries. The roads into Bath were improved in order to bring in more visitors and to make their journey less fatiguing: the turnpike system of roads, their better maintenance and the speeding-up of coach travel brought increasing numbers to other towns of resort and necessitated a corresponding growth in hotel and inn accommodation. By the time that the Regency spas were being built a fifty mile coach journey, which had taken two days in mid-seventeenth century and was still taking a day in summer conditions in 1700, could be accomplished in four hours flat.

Court patronage and aristocratic habits fostered the fashionable phase and the rapid growth of the early spas. The desire, in fact, for a wider field of amusement than London afforded, especially in the summer months, had itself boosted the craze for 'taking the waters'. The increasing wealth and importance—and self-importance—of the middle classes, coupled with the greater accessibility of many places provided by the railway system, encouraged the next phase and new developments. Good living and heavy meals took their toll among the Victorians also: Frank Harris expatiates on the open gluttony and excessive meat-eating at city dinners. For a cure, relief from business and a taste of polite society, what could improve on the health resort and the hydro? With the railway, even such remoter ones as Llandrindod were on the map. The hydro, first popularised in England at Ilkley and Matlock, about mid-century, offered scientific baths of every description. New treatments were constantly devised or imitated and new amenities subsequently added to counter the slight setback which inland resorts were to suffer, when the continental resorts drew away custom by their special facilities, snob appeal and change of scene.

The better conditions of coach travel at home, at the end of the eighteenth century, and the intermission in 'grand tour' travel abroad imposed on the British public by the Napoleonic Wars, were two factors favouring the cult for enjoying picturesque scenery, which caught on after its particular beauties had been publicised by certain naturalists, artists and poets of the period. The English Lake District and Wales, in consequence, came in for tourists' attention. Southey, writing in 1829 of the very many tourists brought to the Land of the Lakes through the migratory habits of the opulent classes, became caustic about the great proportion 'whose object is to get through their undertaking with as little trouble as they can, and whose enquiries are mainly directed to find out what it is *not* necessary for them to see' in taking their degree as 'Lakers'. There were many, of course, who truly enjoyed the opportunities of this 'good and wholesome fashion' and acquired a love of natural scenery which they applied elsewhere.

When railways had penetrated to the threshold of the mountain fastnesses, bringing in a wider social stratum, villages and small towns blossomed into popular places of resort and new ones such as Windermere were created. Wales, especially, was opened up by the railway. The later upsurge of travel in the motor-coach era has led to the danger that the spread of amenities in the various popular centres may spoil for many enjoyment of the natural beauties altogether.

> Each year they come in hundreds full of hope:
> The married pairs with dogs, sharp tweeds, new cars;
> Coach-loads of macs, stiff backs and thinning hair;
> The foreigners with guidebooks, voices, cheques;
> Scouts, couples just engaged, the girls whose chance
> Has almost gone: all seek these lakes, these woods
> And fells that Wordsworth and De Quincey once
> Dowered with fame: a mountain wonderland,
> The 'roots of Heaven', their claim. Since then where else
> Has seemed to hold so true and sure a key
> To peace and happiness, the common dream?
>
> ('Grasmere Revisited')

Such escapes to comparative wildness or solitude as were possible in these picturesque places appeared even more desirable in the context of a country which claimed to be 'the workshop of the world' and its ever-increasing urbanisation. 'The taste for mountain scenery had grown *pari passu* with the Industrial Revolution' (G. M. Trevelyan). As the nineteenth century went on other escapes to the quiet places of nature had increasing appeal. The remaining heathland and ancient forest areas provided comparative paradise for those troubled by the fret of the world, romantically inclined, or in need of a tonic change of air. Lyndhurst and its like reaped the benefit; Epping was the cynosure of city weekenders in the Edwardian pony and trap days.

Hydropathy, which had injected new life into spa resorts in the mid-nineteenth century, finally lost the importance of its role with the advent of the National Health Service and soon thereafter only a handful of spas were left in business. In the noonday of its popularity some resorts had put themselves at risk with over-development in housing and other buildings. Almost all now found themselves with hotels and hydros and amenities liable to become 'white elephants'. The spa idea, of course, was already in decline. Styles of living, habits of eating and spending changed much after World War I; Edwardian middle-class wealth, comfort and leisure—handmaids of hypochondria—rapidly became things of the past. When the support of private patients too was so largely withdrawn, as free National Health treatment of all kinds became available, the problem facing these health-and-pleasure towns was acute. How were they to adapt and how keep their image, more gracious and spacious, it seemed, than the times, still bright— without becoming mere period mausoleums?

The majority have done so, in ways that the following chapters will make clear, although the struggle is still on and other dangers threaten. It is of national, not just local concern, that such artefacts of dignified living and fine exemplars, in many cases, of town planning, are not swamped or denatured by newer developments. So far, more attention has been focused on national parks and natural playgrounds. Enough people care about the countryside for the picturesque resorts to have their fair chance of survival, in spite of 'tin man in his motor-can' and all that follows in his train. Not enough, however, seem to care about the towns and their future, or else make the expression of their care too lamely and too late. Though England today still has much, it has none too much urban beauty.

FREDERICK ALDERSON

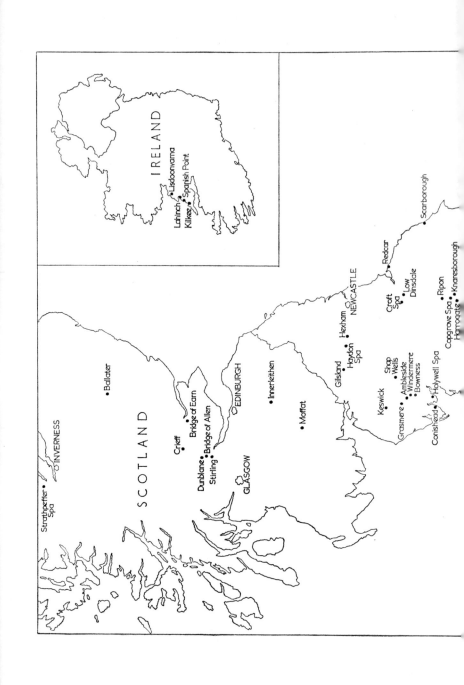

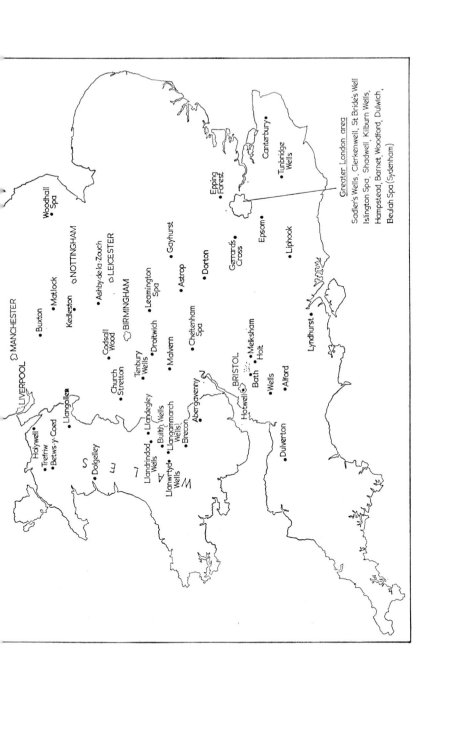

Greater London area

Sadler's Wells, Clerkenwell, St Bride's Well
Islington Spa, Shadwell, Kilburn Wells,
Hampstead, Barnet, Woodford, Dulwich,
Beulah Spa (Sydenham)

Chapter One

EARLY WATERING PLACES

THE BRITISH, as critics of the national character have not failed to remark, tend to take their pleasures sadly: to seek some specious justification for putting self-indulgence before duty; to do one thing whilst calling it something else.

The cult of the inland resort both exemplifies and has satisfied these inclinations. The resorts themselves have perpetuated a special British-ness, surviving still through many changes in style and habit elsewhere. Though easy to dismiss as backwaters, the resorts today are really oases: oases of ways of life and of environment which, by contrast with this century's barren urbanisation, incite less amusement, amaze-ment or ridicule than admiration and envy. The best of them include the best laid-out and preserved of British towns and smaller cities, and encapsulate some of the best of the nation's culture.

What have been generally defined as pleasure resorts with a serious side began as health resorts with a plentiful leavening of pleasure. Of the two main types, the watering place and the picturesque resort, this statement applies more strictly to the former: with the latter health came in, not as raison d'être, but rather as justification. The health-promoting by-products of the picturesque resort, change of air and change of scene, never sounded quite the same compelling note as 'taking the waters'. They are secondary as curative agents, both in time and emphasis, but they have had their importance as handmaids of pleasure. When the concept was firmly established, the ideal health-cum-pleasure resort required, to recommend it, loveliness of landscape, salubrity of climate, interest of neighbourhood and efficacy of springs. Whether the first or the last attribute assumed predominance depended on the individual, his motive, his period, his adviser and his complaint.

The tradition of the inland watering place goes back to Roman times and derives from Roman habits. Although Harrogate can claim to be the first English watering place so designated—being called in 1598 the 'English Spa(w)', after the Belgian town of that name—its springs had been discovered only in 1571, whereas Bath, at the end of the first century AD, was already a resort attracting visitors to its thermal waters from all parts of Roman Britain and the north-western provinces of the Empire. It was neither a military camp nor a city, but a spa: 'In Britain are hot springs furnished luxuriously for human use,' wrote Caius Julius Solinus in the third century, and as Aquae Sulis, with its divinity of the waters Sul Minerva, goddess of medicine, Bath for three hundred years enjoyed Roman patronage.

Buxton (Aquae Arnemetiae) was the one other place in England where the Romans regularly resorted to use the mineral springs and erected buildings for bathers. Like Wiesbaden (Aquae Mattiacorum), whose warm springs the naturalist Pliny credited with retaining their heat for three days, Baden-Baden (Aquae Aureliae) its later rival in popularity, the efficacy of whose waters was also valued by the Romans, the warm springs of Bad Ems (Embasis) and of Badenweiler, where the Romans built a baths complex dedicated to Diana Abnoba, and other continental sites of subsequently famous spas, Aquae Sulis was more than merely a bathing or recuperative centre, and probably Buxton also. Roman baths served as clubs and places of recreation where the poet recited his latest composition, where the athlete sought spectators' admiration with his feats of agility and strength, where jewellers sought their customers and where there were leisurely meetings of friends, gossip, dicing and other games. The business man or minor official working up a good sweat in the exercise hall, the old soldier luxuriating in the hot room and the use of soothing ointments, were also there to enjoy a social occasion. Bath was the archetype for a pattern of English health and pleasure resort many centuries before its re-emergence.

After the Roman withdrawal and Britain's entry into Christendom

Aquae Sulis dropped its reference to both the Roman and an earlier
British divinity. 'Aquae' was preserved as 'Ake' and Bath became for a
time Akeman, a British compound meaning the place known by the
name of Aquae. The old Roman road from London via Marlborough
to Bath is Akeman Street. After the Anglo-Saxon conquest Akeman
turned into Akemanceaster and then, when the virtues of the springs
were rediscovered, into the simple Hoete Bathum. The Saxon chief,
however, who took the place by storm in 577, reduced Roman baths,
temples and all else, along with the town walls, to ruins. As roofs and
walls collapsed and the baths themselves silted up, this imperial bathing
establishment disappeared from view. The town's fame was preserved
—by its medicinal waters and the foundation of a religious house there
in the next century: the resort apparently perished.

In addition to Bath and Buxton, among subsequent English inland
resorts, Droitwich, Ilkley and Matlock were also places of some importance to the Romans. Buxton, as seems likely from its accessibility, may
have attracted more than a local clientele to its waters: several Roman
thoroughfares met there, as can be seen from the Batham Gate, passing
through Fairfield, the Street near Goyt's Bridge, and indications by the
side of the London Road. Droitwich (Salinae) had importance of a
different sort—salt wells derived from beds of rock salt. Within a year
of their landing the Romans built a camp on the heights above these
wells and have left the remains of a villa. It was for the salt industry,
not for brine baths, that they and the Saxons who followed esteemed
Salinae. Again, at Matlock it was not the thermal waters or the petrifying wells whose presence was exploited, but the district's other mineral
wealth—lead, mined there in Roman times. The ancient Nestor mine
can still be viewed. Ilkley (Olicana), although it has at White Wells a
bath of considerable antiquity near a Roman spring, was significant to
that era as a military station at the junction of highways from York to
Ribchester and from Aldborough to Manchester. It was a strategic
point in the establishment of fortified communications across the heart
of the Brigantes' territory—a people resistant to pacification. The fact
that a Roman altar stone dedicated to Verbeia, goddess of the river
Wharfe, was found there really tells no more than that the officer who
dedicated it had a garrison made up of troops from Gaul.

Places with spring waters, not necessarily of special properties, be-came prominent in medieval times. The Romans had valued the practical and external uses of water, both warm and cold. The warm bath, it is said, fell from favour temporarily during the reign of the Emperor Augustus, after it was reported that he had been helped to recovery from a dangerous illness by means of cold ones. Physicians began to promote the cult of the cold bath; citizens of Rome took to it with perhaps more credulity than enthusiasm—until, some time later, the Emperor's son-in-law died after taking one. Of cold water, how-ever, in various springs and fountains, medieval belief emphasised the more miraculous curative powers.

The medieval 'holy well' may have had its special physical properties: they were overlaid by other assumed qualities. Springs and fountains—once the abodes of Gods and spirits, propitiated with offerings in the Roman poet Horace's day ('O Fons Bandusiae') and considered sacred by the Druids—were used by pioneer Christian missionaries to baptise converts and thereafter often became adopted as healing shrines. As Roman springs were identified with a minor deity, a nymph, a goddess of fertility or of healing, so the Christian wells were dedicated to the various saints. The 'magical' assumption that everything associated with a good man is by implication good, and that certain objects, such as the bones of saints, martyrs and conspicuously holy men, possess innate supernatural powers, was readily transferred to such waters. Each disease, moreover, or group of diseases was the responsibility of a special saint.

So, for example, the waters of Little Walsingham, Norfolk, were most popular with sufferers from stomach disorders, while St Madran's Well, Cornwall, traditionally cured sufferers from paralysis. From St Anthony's Well, near Micheldean, Gloucestershire, those bathing in its waters sought relief from erysipelas (St Anthony's fire) and other skin diseases then common. The reputation of the remarkably pure spring waters at Malvern goes equally far back in time, to when the efficacy of its healing virtue was held to be supernatural: the old spring at Great Malvern is dedicated to St Ann, encourager of fertility and a favourite patroness among the saints; the well at Malvern Wells remains the Holy Well. In Glamorganshire the waters of a St Ann's Well were caused to flow out through the stone breasts of the figure of the saint. The curative waters of Glastonbury's Chalice Wells are a special case: Joseph of Arimathea is supposed to have buried the chalice used at the Last Supper under the spring.

Faith on occasions worked wonders and there were recoveries, if only temporary, which appeared to defy rational explanation. After all there were three or four thousand holy wells in Cornwall, Wales and Ireland alone constantly in use. It was not, in such cases, always a matter of applying the well waters, either externally or internally. Pilgrims to St Tecla's Well, Denbighshire, merely circled it three times and then laid their offering on the shrine. A cock or a hen, according to the sufferer's sex, was also carried round the well and then taken into the church by the pilgrim for the night. If the bird died before dawn, it was assumed that St Tecla's disease—the falling sickness—had been transferred to it from the human sufferer.

At Holywell, Flintshire, one of the most celebrated of all places of pilgrimage (visited by Catholic James II and his second queen in August 1696), sufferers from arthritic complaints have found the application of a handkerchief dipped in the ice-cold water of St Winefride's Well miraculously effective when all other 'cures' have failed. One such cure was accompanied, according to its beneficiary the late E. M. Butler, Cambridge Professor of German, by a fountain of water spurting up from the well almost to the roof. St Winefride's has maintained its fame as the Welsh Lourdes, and until recently displayed piles of discarded crutches and other surgical appliances in the shrine belonging to the chapel (rebuilt in 1490 by Lady Margaret Beaufort, mother of Henry VII), despite the fact that the original well went dry and water had to be supplied through pipes by Holywell Corporation. A monthly magazine, the *Holywell Record* appearing in 1897, was devoted to the cause of the conversion of England through the miracles and cures wrought by intercession of the saint, but Frederick Rolfe ('Baron Corvo'), who painted a set of banners for the shrine a year or two before that, had some unsympathetic things to say about Holywell or 'Sewer's End' as his vitriolic pen termed it.

In Scotland renowned springs were not uncommon and were generally resorted to on the first day or the first Sunday of May, a practice which seems to have been derived from the Druidical ceremonies of Beltane: other wells were reported to be most efficacious on the first day of August. Missionaries, when denunciation of well-worship proved vain, merely changed pagan into Christian: St Columba changed a well venerated by the Picts into a holy well. Each well had its guardian saint—St Ninian, for example, for the spring well on the terrace at Stirling: its efficacy was not confined to removing skin or internal ailments in man or woman, but extended to the lower animals. Visitors left their votive offering, perhaps only some portion of yarn or rag, on the margin, and if they benefited, returned to deck the well with flowers on the saint's anniversary.

This habit of making pilgrimages to wells for 'superstitious motives' came in for church censure again and again: it was prohibited by Parliament in Scotland in 1579 and denounced again fifty years later by the Privy Council. It is on record that a Stirling woman, who on the first Sunday in May 1617 had taken a pint of water from Christ's Well for the benefit of a sick relative and left a portion of the invalid's kerchief on a tree by way of oblation, was subjected to kirk session discipline for making use of a superstitious rite. Nevertheless certain holy waters, sometimes of genuine therapeutic value, retained their devotees even when any suggestion of pagan elements or Popish practices caused maximum offence to established religion, and Puritans were eagle-eyed for any remnants of Romish belief. Place names— Bridewell, Elwel, Fritwell—persist in revealing their whereabouts, even if fertility, healing or a glimpse of the future, as they signify, are no longer invoked. And in out-of-the-way places their use may persist also; people in Bellingham, Northumberland, still like to draw water from St Cuthbert's Well, long supposed to have healing powers.

The naming of wells and fountains after particular saints also continued. In the writer's village in Westmorland the stone embrasures of roadside springs are inscribed to St James, St John and St Margaret (virgin and martyr of Antioch invoked by women in childbirth): their waters, however, have been labelled by the UDC as unfit for drinking purposes. Whether they were considered curative originally is not certain. It does not follow, of course, from the veneration of wells and from pilgrimages or local visits to them that there was a spa resort in the making there, or that one should have been expected to develop at some later stage. Some of the more successful spas did develop out of a very long magical or religious past and the changes of attitude to the 'waters' from paganism to Christianity, and then, after the Reformation, to secular rationalisation are clearly marked: but various fortuitous factors are involved in addition to the properties of the water and their timely recognition.

Bath, to return to the exemplar, suffered vicissitudes that included a second sacking and burning at the time of King Rufus's struggle against the rising in favour of his brother Robert; restoration by the first Bishop of Bath and Wells, a physician and royal chaplain who was permitted to purchase Bath from Rufus for 500 marks, with abbey, mint and baths included; then again decay, after a foreign bishop-lord of Bath had exchanged his seat for Glastonbury, in Cœur de Lion's time, and the city had reverted to the crown. At length, in 1590, a new charter was given by Elizabeth I which enlarged the powers and area of the corporation and restored to it ownership of the hot springs. They were again becoming popular and had acquired a reputation for the healing of leprosy and skin diseases.

The following year the queen, on a visit to her godson Sir John Harrington at Kelveston, herself visited Bath, but came away with a poor impression. 'Their common sewer, which before stood in an ill place, stands now in no place, for they have not any at all; which for a towne so plentifully served of water, in a country so well provided of stone, in a place resorted unto so greatly, methinke,' wrote Harrington to Lord Burleigh, 'seemeth an unworthie and dishonourable thing.'

Royal notice, however, for any place with natural advantages, was a sure fillip to its advancement. 'Since her Highnesse being there the citie hath wonderfully beautified itselfe in fine houses for victualling and lodging.' Bath, if funds were honestly applied, continued Sir John, could be made instead of 'an unsavorie town a most sweet town'. The remark is pregnant with significance for the development of quite a number of English inland resorts, whose natural advantages required only scientific recognition to bring them in due course to royal notice.

Chapter Two

FASHION-SETTERS

OF THE two inland watering places which can be regarded as fashion-setters (in the double sense), Bath and Tunbridge Wells, it was the latter and nearer to London that flowered first. A lengthy visit of the King of Denmark and his court to the court of King James I in 1606 involved English courtiers in riotous living on such a scale as to send many post-haste into the country to recuperate, as soon as the royal visit was over. One of them, the third Baron North, stayed at Eridge with his friend Lord Bergavenny; on returning from there to London via Tonbridge he observed a pool of reddish water from a spring with 'a ruddy ochreous track'. It put him in mind of the waters at the resort of Spa, Belgium. Lord North took a sample of the spring for analysis by his physician, who found in it iron and other medicinal elements. Subsequently a course of these chalybeate waters improved the courtier's state of health—he was possibly consumptive—so much that other members of the nobility followed his example for cures from various excesses, staying at the houses of their friends in the neighbourhood. When, in 1630, Queen Henrietta Maria came to drink the waters, recuperating after the birth of her son Charles II, a royal encampment was set up for her and her retinue on the present open common.

Scientific analysis—secular rationalisation—of its waters, in that age of excited physical enquiry, was one significant factor in the promotion of 'The Wells', as the place became known. Spa therapy came in as the

mystical water cure was played down: the prevalence of an almost exclusively meat and wheat diet and excessive port and sherry drinking
among the well-to-do made some type of spa treatment advisable. The
cult was a sop to hypochondria and an excuse for taking a holiday, or
making a change in the continuous round of amusement demanded by
the later Stuarts, and not unnaturally, where exploitation of human
weakness for gain was so inviting, it abounded in 'empiricks' and
quackery. The chief springs of pure and soft water at Tunbridge, 'very
quick springs from steele and iron mines', were soon to have wells
sunk to them and surrounding pavements and railings added, as the
wealthy and fashionable continued to flock there for cures, especially
for colic.

The other important factor in any resort's development was the
building of lodgings and amenities for visitors attractive enough to encourage their stay. The early air of rusticity and the primitive refreshment huts, market booths and taverns, which gave a *fête champêtre*
atmosphere to the cure, was its by nature transitional. Eight years after
Queen Henrietta Maria's visit, the ground beside the wells was levelled,
trees were planted to form a parade, known then as the Lower and Upper
Walks (subsequently developed into the famous 'Pantiles'), and other
building was in progress. But when King Charles II and Queen Catherine first came to Tunbridge Wells, twenty-five years after that, in
1663, their retinue still had to live in tents and pavilions on the Common, although there was a house for the royal couple. Two years later
King and court sought refuge there from the Plague. The Walks were
established as a fashionable promenade for the Restoration elite and
'The Wells' became a subject for complaint, described by the Puritans
as 'waters of scandal' where love's empire never so flourished. The
first arcade of shops and houses there was destroyed by a fire in 1687.

Other royal patrons of 'The Wells' included the king's brother,
James, who as Duke of York stayed with his family and visited the
High Rocks beyond Broadwater Forest. Queen Catherine of Braganza
sought a cure for her sterility both at Tunbridge and at Bath. Princess
(later Queen) Anne, daughter of James II, was another frequent visitor:
when, in the summer of 1697, her young son the Duke of Gloucester
slipped and fell on one of the grass Walks, she complained—and gave

£100 to have it paved, with the square baked pantiles that have given the Upper Walk its present name. The restored, lime-tree-shaded colonnade, paved now with Purbeck flagstones—only fifteen of the original pantiles remain—and its shops give the town its distinctive attraction. The 'Queen's Grove' was planted on the Common by the townspeople in her honour.

By the end of the century a foreign traveller in England, Henri Misson, observed that 'the pretence of these waters brings together vast numbers of people of both sexes that are in very good health'. At that time Tunbridge was the most fashionable resort: its shops, coffee houses, piazza, lottery houses, and bowling greens on Mount Zion and Mount Ephraim were frequented by company that, although numerous, was always select, since pleasure-seekers predominated. Life at 'The Wells' in contemporary opinion was delicious. Tunbridge being the same distance from London as Fontainebleau from Paris, it was, in season, the general rendezvous of all the gay and handsome of both sexes, where constraint was banished and familiarity established on first acquaintance. The company lodged in small houses, straggling and separated from each other, but met each morning to stroll on the Walks, to drink the waters and to buy their lace, gloves, stockings and so on at the long row of shops, or their provisions from the market on the other side. Young, fresh-faced country girls with clean linen, small straw hats and neat shoes and stockings sold game, vegetables, fruit and flowers there. Some of the things that visitors admired and bought in the shops were tea-caddies and boxes, tooth-picks, and trays covered with mosaic veneers in local wood and superscribed with such mottoes as

> When this you see
> Remember me

—the delicate, patterned Tunbridge Ware. In the evening they could dance in the open air at the bowling green on lawns softer and smoother than the finest carpet.

When rich patients, who sought a more welcome alternative to the contemporary medical regime of purging, dosing and bleeding, threatened to make Islington Spa into the 'new Tunbridge Wells', the older spa countered by denouncing Islington's waters as sham, concocted of cow turds and steel dust, and its well as 'new-vamped'. But 'how negligent and extravagant they are at all these places of dissipation', remarked a visitor in 1768, who had seen everything at 'The Wells', drunk his glass of water, walked to the celebrated rocks—the finest natural curiosity he had seen—and slept at the Sussex tavern.

Building, in the manner to which mid-eighteenth century visitors to Bath were already growing accustomed, came later to Tunbridge Wells or not at all. There were the Pantiles, with their 'musick' balcony and tradesmen's elegant window displays under steep tiled eaves, and a broad parade under the row of trees. Here 'rich Cloths, Jewels and Beauty dazzle the Eyes from one end of the Range to the other'. Near the entrance stood the Church of King Charles the Martyr, opened in 1678, with its beautiful baroque plaster ceiling by Henry Doogood and John Wetherill (its wooden cupola and clock date from 1759). There was a Pump Room (now demolished, although the chalybeate spring still has a clientele); and there was a theatre on the Lower Walk, opened in 1802. But it was not until the 1820s that the town flowered architecturally. This was more than two generations after Richard 'Beau' Nash, coming from Bath as Master of Ceremonies in 1735, had turned the fashionable health resort into a fashionable pleasure resort which nearly everyone of social importance visited, with Garrick, Reynolds, Richardson, Mrs Thrale and Colley Cibber among other artistic celebrities. The main credit for this flowering belongs to Decimus Burton, who also designed the Ionic screen at Hyde Park Corner and several terraces at Regent's Park, and laid out some of the best squares and terraces at St Leonards; and to his brother James. Decimus designed Holy Trinity Church in local sandstone, consecrated in 1829: together with James he was responsible for Calverley Crescent and the informal 'picturesque' Calverley Park, to the east of the Mount Pleasant Road. The Walk was built in the 1830s. Calverley Crescent, with its iron balconies at first-floor level and its colonnade of slender columns, was obviously designed for shops, but is now a system of terraced houses, whose darkened stone detracts somewhat from their conscious air of distinction. The town's leading hotel, the Calverley, overlooking Calverley Grounds and commanding fine views of Ashdown Forest, was formerly Calverley House, where the young Princess Victoria used to stay in the 1830s when visiting with her mother, the Duchess of Kent, at her 'dear Tunbridge Wells'. By this time the town was entering its third phase, as a favoured residential resort.

Even though it possessed no architectural heritage to compare with that of Bath (or those of Buxton and Cheltenham), 'The Wells', with its large triangular common between the London Road and Mount Ephraim, its unusual sandstone outcrops, its wide streets and pavements like Mount Pleasant, its charming groups of Regency and early Victorian houses in Mount Zion and Cumberland Walk (some with ammonite capitals by the Brighton architect Amon Henry Wilds), its shopping precinct and its general feeling of space, light, cheerfulness and greenery, continued to attract people of discernment and leisure, as well as hypochondriacs. It is one of the English towns 'which by tradition and convention may be visited for the pure pleasure of visiting them'.

The world of fashion switched its allegiance to Brighton. Sea-water as a cure or tonic (first advocated by Dr Richard Russell in 1753) and the sea resorts affected some of those 'prudent grandmammas and modern belles' who had once been

> Content with Bristol, Bath and Tunbridge Wells:
> When health requir'd it would consent to roam,
> Else more attached to pleasures found at home—

but older traditions still persisted. Tunbridge's theatre eventually became a Corn Exchange in 1843, but the Royal Sussex Assembly Rooms, also on the Lower Walk (later the Royal Victoria and Sussex Hotel), remained a centre of resort well up to the middle of the century, before becoming a furniture repository, the 'Pantechnicon', in 1880.

The sprightly Miss Twinkleton, proprietress of a seminary for young ladies (in Dickens's *Edwin Drood*) enjoyed her season at 'The Wells' and the attentions there of a 'certain finished gentleman', ' "Foolish Mr Porter" '. Thackeray lived in a square Georgian house, across the common from Mount Ephraim, and added lustre to this assembly room and circulating library period by revivifying it in his novels especially *The Virginians*. Queen Victoria's visits with Prince Albert, and George

Meredith's, in their different ways, echoed a quality or gave a tone that the coming of the railway in 1846 had tended to dilute. Concerts and subscription balls in the Assembly Rooms, with a Master of the Rooms wearing knee-breeches; the occasional visit there of a ventriloquist or a mesmerist, an Infant Phenomenon or a professor with an orrery; a special sale of fancy china; a public reading by a popular novelist; visits to the library for the latest romances of the Minerva Press; church parade or service at a dissenting chapel, such as the Congregational Doric temple in Mount Pleasant: walks across the Common to the Wellington Rocks or the Toad Rocks at Rusthall— these were some of the Victorian resort's diversions. Not of the kind, one supposes, to put even the puritan out of countenance or reinvoke comment like 'sink of iniquity' and 'parade of wanton dalliances' apropos the Pump Room. Among favourite culinary specialities were ortolans and fresh mackerel.

One of the gracious hotels on Mount Ephraim, among Regency and early Victorian villas, was surmounted by a great lion and unicorn. Another, in the nineties, advertised itself as patronised by his Grace the late Duke of Wellington and as commanding, from its position nearly five hundred feet above sea-level, distant views into forest scenery 'unsurpassed in the Ardennes for the wild grandeur of their surroundings'. At this period it had been remodelled, redrained, redecorated and refurnished (by Warings) and was warmed in winter 'by an elaborate system of radiators'. Whereas the high ground, high sunshine record and dry climate were enough to attract summer visitors, hotels like these encouraged their residential stay. The list of royal patrons, meanwhile, extended to Queen Mary, King George VI and the present Queen Mother. For the last sixty years the borough has been known as the Royal Tunbridge Wells—by gracious command of King Edward VII.

As an inland resort, in the Garden of England fruit and hop-growing country, about one hour's journey from either London or the coast, Tunbridge Wells today lives less on its past than does its greater rival Bath. It flourishes as a smart shopping and residential centre: many who came for a limited stay have returned to live there. Visitors may take their glass of sparkling water on the Pantiles, whose Victorian and other facades add variety to the colonnades; but they are more likely to linger over the rich and various displays of antiques. The town has become virtually a headquarters for this trade: it is nothing out of the ordinary for buyers from the USA to stroll through for a couple of hours, look at ten or a dozen shops and spend $50,000. The fine antiquarian bookshops, the cricket fixtures on the famous Kent County ground the Nevill (the town club began its existence in 1782) are other lures. One is impressed here by the immaculate style and the mannerly crowd. There is much else to attract the spectator, the browser, the loiterer in the sun.

The town whose local industry gave its name to Tunbridge Ware—which was notably developed, with mosaic pictures, in the nineteenth century—still concentrates on specialities of unusual quality. The means of adaptation from a fashionable past to a firmly based economic future has been the developing of light industrial estates, for such things as spectacle frames and lenses, perfumes, electrical components and for colour printing. 'Do well, doubt not' is the borough motto.

Bath, turned by Beau Nash into a kind of national finishing school, owed its renascence as a fashionable centre to visits paid by Queen Anne. In the mid-seventeenth century complaints were still being made that its streets were dung-hills, slaughter-houses and pigsties and that its baths were bear-gardens, where passers-by pelted the bathers with dead cats and dogs. Roughs and adventurers with swords and bludgeons gave offence to ladies on the promenades: the medieval city consisted of a maze of only four or five hundred houses intersected by mean and narrow thoroughfares, crowded within the old wall. Gentlemen who visited the springs had to sleep in rooms no better than garrets; dining-room floors were coloured brown to hide the dirt, with a wash made of soot and small beer. Sedan chairmen were extraordinarily 'rude and boorish'.

The visits of Anne, first as Princess and private visitor, then in 1702 with a royal welcome as Queen of England, did much to focus the attention of the fashionable world on Bath. What the court did and said and wore were endless themes for conversation and imitation: those whose aim was to follow fashion gazed courtwards in concentric circles. Whereas London society could be entered only by those in recognised public positions and provincial society was virtually ruled by local squires, in Bath, once given the cachet of royal presence, votaries of fashion found a less exclusive meeting place. Here objects and manners for imitation could be freely displayed, while those not privileged to enter the royal portals could take for their pattern the favoured few. So the city became a rallying place of 'good company'; and when those who had come for health only were followed by those who came for modes and manners and pleasure, its accommodation was thronged and its confines became too narrow for the numbers of its visitors.

The first Pump Room was built in 1706, the first (Harrison's) Assembly Rooms in 1708. Balls at this time were given at the Town Hall and cost half a guinea a ticket—for the privilege of small gentry enjoying themselves with the great ones of the land. A theatre was built in 1720. It was not, however, until the two men who rose to the city's emergency, and their own fortunes, came upon the scene that a resort arose, pre-eminent in both style and architecture. Then the Georgian outgrowth (begun under Queen Anne) gathered such momentum that it far outran the ancestral city.

Resorts have been created by landowners, by speculators, by physicians and by railway companies. Bath was especially fortunate in finding together a far-sighted, business-like quarry owner and a man with big ideas and imagination in handling stone. Ralph Allen, after beginning as a post office assistant in Cornwall, moved to Bath and quickly obtained the position of postmaster there, as a reward for his supplying valuable information to General Wade during the '15 rebellion. While still in his twenties he began, at his own expense, the reform of the whole English mail system. The profitable results of his conspicuous success were invested in land and in the quarries of the remarkably durable Bath stone at Combe Down. John Wood, a Yorkshireman, born about 1704 and educated in the Renaissance School of Architecture, was induced to come to Bath, probably by Allen who saw the prospect of combining the projected development of the city and of his stone quarries, with the assistance of the right man.

Wood's first job was the addition of a wing, in 1726–7, to Allen's town house, used as a post office. After completing St John's Hospital about the same year he next began the building of Queen's Square—named in honour of Queen Caroline—architecturally influenced by Inigo Jones. So commenced a 'piece of town planning unique in Europe' (Pevsner) which was to give Bath, instead of the cramped squalor and 'streets narrow, uneven and unpleasant' (Evelyn) of a 'very small city, round, compact, lying in low ground' (Yonge), space and symmetry combined with solidity, utility and elegance. Wood's squares, circles and crescents, developed in the Palladian manner, amounted in fact to a new and model city, comparable with Florence. Queen's Square was completed in 1735, with a terrace on the north side of revolutionary design, intended to look like a Palladian palace: its rusticated ground floor, pedimented centrepiece, strong emphasis in the form of attic storeys at either end and its giant Corinthian order uniting first and second floors, gave it a monumental illusion. In the meantime Wood designed Prior Park with a bold Corinthian portico for Ralph Allen, a splendid advertisement for the beauty of Bath stone and one of the grandest country seats of the period: its cost was £240,000. He then went on to the building of the North and South Parades (formerly called the 'Grand Parade' and the 'Royal Forum') just beyond the city wall. Although John Wood senior did not live to complete his urban layout—Gay Street, the Circus, Brock Street and the Royal Crescent—his son, also John Wood, carried out his work.

The first stone of the Royal Circus, named in honour of George II, was laid by Wood the elder in 1754. Its design recalled Vespasian's amphitheatre at Rome, turned inside out, complete with superimposed Doric, Ionic and Corinthian orders. Divided into three parts only it presented a group of buildings in circular form to a spectator from any one of the entrances, a striking and successful feature. Brock Street linked the Circus to the Royal Crescent, built entirely by the younger Wood, and reverting to the Ionic order which passed through the two upper storeys in true Palladian manner. Built between 1767 and 1775, it contains thirty houses in a semi-ellipse, with a continuous cornice supported by a hundred and fourteen columns—a magnificent pile enhanced by the great open spaces of lawn before it. It has been termed the finest crescent in Europe—the slightly later and smaller one at Buxton which resembles it being called the finest building of the kind in England! The new Assembly Rooms, just east of the Circus, were also designed by the younger Wood, together with some surrounding streets and the (old) Royal Bath or Hot Bath, in 1777, at the end of Bath Street. His father's chief public works in the city were the Mineral Water Hospital, begun in 1738, and the Wiltshire Assembly Rooms.

Although they, father and son, were the foremost in establishing this resort in its remarkable setting of integrated architecture, the Woods were not Bath's only master builders. 'There is nothing in London equal to the Circus, all the great streets are remarkably clean and neat' (Neville): Milsom Street, the Regent Street of Bath, but formerly residential, runs for part of its length parallel to Gay Street and includes the Octagon Chapel (now a public hall) at its lower end: both of these were designed by Thomas Lightoler. A group of the houses have also their Corinthian columns and pediments. The Paragon, where Jane Austen once lodged with her mother, is nearer the river and came, not unworthily of its name, from a plumber and painter turned architect, Thomas Atwood.

Pulteney Street, where Mr and Mrs Allen (*Northanger Abbey*) had comfortable lodgings, was laid out on lines proposed by Robert Adam: it is 1,100 feet in length with a distance of 100 feet from house to house. The design was completed by Thomas Baldwin, a former employee of Attwood, but the three-arch Pulteney Bridge over the Avon, built in 1771, is wholly Adam's. It echoes the charm of the Ponte Vecchio. To cross the bridge and promenade by Laura Place along the length of this street to the Sydney Gardens is both to see and to feel what spacious, dignified town-planning really means. Bath Street, with the unique feature of an Ionic colonnade on both sides, to provide a covered way for patients' exercise and for shopping, is also Baldwin's work and is little altered; so too are the colonnade added to the enlarged Pump Room, in 1785, on the west end, the rebuilt Cross Bath and the Guildhall Banqueting Room. This whole area may remind the traveller of such Roman cities as Ephesus or Jerash, whose stone streets and colonnades have been remarkably restored, exemplars dazzling in the sun.

Page 33 (*above*) The Pantiles, Tunbridge Wells; (*below*) Royal Crescent, Bath

Page 34   Bath Abbey, Abbey churchyard and Pump Room

The Lansdown Crescent by John Palmer, who designed the portico attached to the north side of the Pump Room, and Camden Crescent (originally Place) were other notable additions to Bath's housing made towards the close of the century. The Lansdown for many years marked the upper fringe of residential building and seemed to crown the beautiful city which it overlooked. Few places outside Italy could compete with the panorama of these stately houses in tier upon tier of crescents and terraces, running uphill and revealing unbroken lines of facades in honey-coloured Bath stone: 'it looks like a city that has been cast in a mould all at once' a French visitor in 1811 remarked. 'The mile-long, unbroken ribbon of noble terraces running from Broad Street past Bladud Buildings, the Paragon and trailing north-eastwards through Grosvenor along the London road is something unprecedented and unsurpassed in urban planning' (James Lees-Milne). And like Milsom Street, where General Tilney's (*Northanger Abbey*) family stayed, it seems that most of the residential streets in Bath were, from the first, occupied for lodgings as much as for private dwellings.

Its Roman heritage as health centre and its neo-classical splendour as a city, important though they were, have not been the only major factors in creating Bath's fame as a resort. Travellers in the seventeenth and early eighteenth centuries came for the saline waters (discovered in this century to be radio-active): they were reputed to cure ennui and to revitalise the passions and, in later theory, to be efficacious in cases of debility, obesity, gout, digestive disorders, orthopaedic conditions and rheumatism. Evelyn bathed in the Cross Bath and considered the King's Bath the fairest in Europe, as it was also the most fashionable. Pepys, a decade or so later, found the King and Queen's Bath full of a mixed sort, of good and bad, and the Cross almost exclusively for the gentry: 'The manner pretty enough, only methinks it cannot be clean to go so many into the same water.' He got a boy to dive into the King's Bath for a shilling, paid his two women guides five shillings and a woman to lay his footcloth one shilling. Yonge visited each bath, the Cross, the King's and Queen's and the Leopard's Bath: in each he saw the crutches hung up of those who, having been cripples, went away cured and able to walk without them. Celia Fiennes, journeying through England a few years after Yonge, found that the baths made the town unpleasant, the air thick and hot by their steam (water issued at 119°F). She compared conveyances with those of the company that resorted there to drink or bathe in the summer. All morning they used chairs of bayes (baize) to carry them to the bath; later in the day sedan chairs to carry them on visits. The only new thing that she noticed when she came a dozen years later (in 1698) was a hall for balls and dancing.

Had any of these travellers been able to visit Bath again, after another half century, they would have scarcely noticed the conditions of the baths for the evidence of a new code of conduct and manners. Richard 'Beau' Nash (1674–1761) had been on the scene. The Pump Room, built under his auspices, soon after his arrival in 1704, and the Assembly Rooms became instruments for welding an inchoate throng of would-be fashionable visitors into a social edifice, balanced, graded, harmonious as the new architecture. 'He first diffused a desire for society and easiness of address among a whole people formerly censured for their reserved awkwardness' is Goldsmith's tribute. How was it done? By first establishing his own personality, manner and appearance: assets which had not had sufficient scope previously, either at Oxford, in the Army or in the Middle Temple; by offering advice, suggestions and plans of improved amenities; by a wittily devised code of social and sumptuary rules and by constantly keeping transgressors in mind of them; by the support of his friend, Dr Oliver, of biscuit fame; finally by the universal esteem and authority that attended his own social success.

The curriculum of Bath life for visitors was itself a framework for conduct: the regular succession of elegant amusements brought everyone into 'the swim'. They went for their bath in King's or Cross Bath between 6 and 9am, to the music of flutes, fiddles or harp:

> 'Twas a glorious sight to behold the fair sex
> All wading with gentlemen up to their necks.

(The gentlemen were in canvas waistcoats and drawers, the ladies in robes adorned with yellow ribbons, or jackets and petticoats of brown linen with chip hats—and each with a floating tray for handkerchief, nosegay, snuff box.) Then they breakfasted in their lodging or the

Assembly Rooms, took their three glasses of water in the Pump Room until 11am (the glasses, of different sizes, were ranged in order before the pumper behind the bar and the drinker pointed to whichever size he chose): after which many attended morning service in the Abbey. (Use of Bath waters internally began, on the recommendation of Charles II's chief physician, Sir Alexander Frazer, at the time of the visit by the King in 1663.) Riding, walking, driving on the parades or, later, on Royal Crescent, or window-shopping at milliners', booksellers' or toy-men's, occupied the time until dinner at 2 or 2.30pm, after which one frequented the Pump Room or Orange Grove. Tea, at about 5pm at the Assembly Rooms or in the Spring Gardens was the prelude to the evening visit, ball, concert, theatre or play in the gaming room, where gambling was public and properly organised up to the middle of the century. Nash's income came largely from the cut he took of the banker's winnings and his own successful gambling.

The Nash code of manners posted in the Pump Room gave to this round of pleasure a certain dignity and feeling of importance. 'That a visit of ceremony at first coming, and another at going away, are all that is expected or desired by ladies of quality and fashion—except impertinents' was one dictum; 'That gentlemen of fashion never appearing in a morning before ladies in caps and gowns show breeding and respect'; 'That no gentleman give his ticket for the balls to any but gentlewomen. NB unless he has none of his acquaintance'; 'That no gentleman or lady takes it ill that another dances before them—except such as have no pretence to dance at all'; 'That all whisperers of scandal be taken for their authors'; 'That no person take it ill that anyone goes to another's play, or breakfast, and not theirs—except captious by nature'; these and the other witty pin-pricks began to penetrate. Nash could forbid gentlemen smoking their churchwardens in public rooms, ban the wearing of white aprons at assemblies even by duchesses —or riding boots by noblemen at dances, discourage the wearing of swords, refuse dancing extensions beyond the fixed hour of eleven, even to princesses—and get away with it. He could, as *Tom Jones* shows, try to protect innocence when 'the Bath talked loudly' almost 'roared' against some pretty miss. He was also instrumental in opening a subscription list for keeping the Pump Room clean and in order and for the maintenance of a band, in promoting a fund to pave and light the streets, in inducing the Corporation to improve the suburbs and in having the Abbey Bells rung (for a fee of half a guinea) whenever a stage coach arrived with noble or important visitors, a practice copied later at Brighton.

All these innovations added to the graces of life in Bath—for which the phrase 'national finishing school' (instead of 'national hospital') became more than merely a quip. Bath was the place in England to enjoy good health and turn it to account: even invalids seemed to have none of the illnesses which spoiled enjoyment. All was gaiety, good humour and diversion. No doubt it attracted those who knew no other criterion of greatness but the ostentation of wealth—planters, negro-drivers, hucksters and factors from the East Indies, usurers, brokers and jobbers, the wives and daughters of wartime contractors and commis-saries who suddenly found themselves translated into a state of affluence. The slightest indisposition served them as pretext to insist on being conveyed to Bath 'where they may hobble country-dances and cotillions among lordlings, 'squires, counsellors and clergy, these delicate crea-tures from Bedfordbury, Butcher-Row, Crutched-Friars and Botolph Lane' (Smollett). But if they came without the least idea of propriety and decorum, at least they helped to swell the demand for elegant apartments and new houses, while some may have recommended better taste to others even by their own absurd extravagance. One thing is certain: as Bath's celebrity grew its commodities fetched extortionate prices and the costs of housekeeping soared. 'Here now is a mushroom of opulence, who pays a cook seventy guineas a week for furnishing him with one meal a day . . . a negro-driver from Jamaica paid over-night to the master of one of the rooms, sixty-five guineas for tea and coffee to the company, [then] left Bath next morning in such ob-scurity that not one of his guests had the slightest idea of his person, or even made the least enquiry about his name' (Smollett).

Instead of being a satellite of London, as Tunbridge Wells tended to be, Bath became an alternative London in the west—a fashionable centre for the well-to-do community of the eighteenth century and, on many counts, a major civilising influence. It was better suited than the unwieldy, conglomerate metropolis for shaping society; its architecture, whose appreciation then was part of a gentleman's education, could do much to turn a civil man into a cultured one. A Horace Walpole might say of it, after mid-century, 'These watering-places that mimic a capital add vulgarisms and familiarities of their own that I am not young enough to take up with', but few were his equal as exquisites. Earlier Alexander Pope had been content to have his whole day shared by the Pump assemblies, the walks, the chocolate houses, raffling shops, medleys and so on, and to 'endeavour like all awkward fellows to become agreeable by imitation'. In its heyday, towards the end of the century, the throng and press of people was like that of a capital, both in the streets and at the assemblies. 'Everybody acquainted with Bath may remember the difficulties of crossing Cheap St at this point (opposite Union Passage). Never a day passes in which parties of ladies, however important their business, whether in quest of pastry, millinery or even of young men, are not detained on one side or the other by carriages, horsemen or carts' (Jane Austen)—or by a gig driven vehemently along a bad pavement. There was music in the Pump Room every morning, cotillions every forenoon in the rooms, balls twice a week, and concerts every other night, besides private assemblies and parties without number. The company met for chat or cards and tea-drinking in the two public rooms, Simpson's and Wiltshire's, each alternate evening. The crowds in the Pump Room were almost insupportable: at full season the ballrooms were so packed that spectators like Catherine Morland (*Northanger Abbey*) saw nothing but the high feathers of some of the ladies as they took turn in the interminable succession of minuets then predominant. At tea-drinking (given to the company, on occasion, by an individual for the sake of éclat) one was fortunate even to share a table. Bath, it is true, although 'the very centre of racket and dissipation', compared with London had little variety—as everybody found out every year, it soon grew tiresome; but, having come for six weeks, they often lengthened their stays to ten or twelve.

Bath's rich patronage also exerted influence on artists and craftsmen, both locally and in London. City and provincial goldsmiths, for example, found inspiration in the demand for brilliant display and luxurious living among the leading families and surrounding stately homes. Table services, with numerous individual pieces like tureens, terrines, bowls, domed covers to keep things hot, wine-coolers and coffee pots were an innovation especially popular in Bath, along with the appropriate table silver, centrepieces and candelabra. Fine houses were filled with furniture, required to be elegant as well as comfortable, or to have a restrained perfection of form such as the great English designers, Chippendale and Hepplewhite, supplied towards the century's end. Modish trifles, far removed from Tunbridge Ware, were poured out by silversmiths and goldsmiths—Bath rings, smelling bottles, snuff boxes, patch boxes, walking-stick handles, watches and their elaborate pendants and chain. Local tradesmen had 'never had it so good'; it comes as no surprise that shops of quality and antique dealers of wide repute abound in Bath today.

Of society itself, the civilising hub and symbol of the higher life was for many years Prior Park—some half-hour's walk from the city centre. The impression of magnificent opulence and power given by Ralph Allen's house was matched by the brilliance of the company he attracted there—Pitt, Bolingbroke, Arbuthnot, Fielding, Gay, Pope. The 'Squire Allworthy' of Fielding derives from the character of Allen, 'a gentleman of Somersetshire who might well be called the favourite of both nature and fortune', who takes his place along with Nash and Wood as the third moulder of Bath into 'an epitome of the century'. After Nash's death in 1761 and Allen's in 1764 the centre of the group and the masterhand of ceremony were lacking, but their example carried over even though Bath society became more stratified —with its 'blue-stockings', Parnassians at Batheaston and chapel folk of Lady Huntingdon's connexion (for whom the Vineyards chapel was built). Among its later figures were the Sheridans, Thomas—Dr Johnson's 'Sherry'—and Richard Brinsley (who set *The Rivals* there), his wife Elizabeth Linley, first singer of her day, the bright, particular star Mrs Siddons, Gainsborough and Lawrence, Chatham, William Herschel and, of course, the 'Bath cats', Mrs Thrale, Miss Burney and Miss Austen. There was rarely a novel or memoir written in the eighteenth century in which the mode of Bath life and its exemplars did not have mention. And it was the custom, well into the nineteenth, for leaders of intellectual life, painters and actors, novelists, poets, dramatists, statesmen and divines, explorers and soldiers to spend at least part of each year in this society, up to the time of Landor and Lytton. Where else could one have such daily opportunities of seeing the most remarkable characters of the community in their natural attitudes and true colours, descended from their pedestals, divested of their formal draperies, undisguised by art and affectation? Where else could one find the general mixture of all degrees assembled in public rooms without distinction of rank or fortune? The very chaos of the company was a source of infinite amusement.

Just as there had been early critics who saw the development of Bath as fantastical—after its Circus 'a pretty bauble contrived for show' and Crescent, anticipating a Star followed by all the signs of the Zodiac exhibited in its architecture, so to some later ones the old pavements and colonnades, the trim stone houses, porches, arched doorways, window mouldings, iron railings, lamp holders and 'link' extinguishers gave the city the air of a monument or museum. Dickens thought the whole place looked like a cemetery, which the dead had succeeded in rising from and taking over, having built streets of their old gravestones. He affected to hate the sight of the bygone assembly rooms and the Bath chairs trundling dowagers about the streets. Perhaps one of his readings there had not gone well or he missed the old dinners with Landor. His animadversion for the 'mouldy old roosting place' is more personal than John Wesley's who considered it 'Satan's headquarters', where the devil took it ill to be attacked. Even before the decline of Bath as a social centre, about 1830, there had been derogatory comments from sharp eyes and pens: though at its full brilliance in the Napoleonic era, the combination of rigid etiquette 'more stiff, formal and oppressive than the etiquette of a German elector', and elegant amusement staled for the more discerning. Private parties were preferred to the public amusements and affectation of fashion among the beau monde. Celebrities grew tired of the crush. 'Went at night to the Harmonic: very full room: at least 300 persons. Never was so stared at in my life before . . . During the ball was stared at on all sides without mercy. In such a place as Bath any little lion makes a stir' (Moore). Moore, *not* a 'little lion', was also aware of having created a sensation throughout the whole establishment when he gave a signed cheque for the purchase of carpets and chimneypieces in Milsom Street. Cultivated people were expressing a poor opinion of Bath society: even Queen's Square had lost tone. 'None of your Queen's Squares for us,' says a character in *Persuasion*, whose author had gone to live there in 1797. Bath, in fact, had fulfilled its role, that of refining manners and educating taste, until taste grew independent and veered in other directions. And all the gay birds of passage had taken their flight, not as of old to Bristol-well, Tunbridge, Scarborough, Harrowgate, but to the new Brighton.

The great Roman Bath, the greatest architectural monument of Roman Britain, has of course attracted, since its uncovering less than a century ago, innumerable visitors to Bath; as also has Bath Abbey, restored a decade ago, whose walls are covered with no fewer than 614 memorial tablets of great historical interest. The tender browns and greys of the stone-built city evoke its Augustan past. But it was not only history and its reminders which drew the generals and admirals of renown, from Lord Nelson to Lord Roberts, to settle in Bath with their families when its days of high fashion were over, or continued to make it 'a swarming city filled with the unique ringing of bells' in the diarist Kilvert's time, as he bought six pairs of kid gloves at 1s 6d a pair at Hampers; or in that later Georgian era when, between the endless round of amusements, 'all day long electric trams whiz passengers to outlying and uplying suburbs, from which the walks are fresh and charming'. Not only those who came with their doctor's prescription, took their bath tickets and paid for their visitor's ticket—a kind of surtax—giving entrée to Pump Room and gardens, concerts and entertainments, sought out Bath. The mild climate, beautiful neighbourhood, choice of well-built houses and hotels, the gardens and parks made it the resort also of those who sought to combine urban dignity, comfort and above all taste in their permanent abode. The sense of Bath as an alternative to London was re-emphasised when some six thousand Admiralty and other Government servants were centred there after 1940—almost as many as the personnel of the city's combined medical and other professions, or the total of hotel, shop and restaurant employees, the third major ingredient in its active population. Like London it suffered also under the Luftwaffe, in the so-called Baedeker raids.

Bath has its industrial area, paradoxically tucked away in the west end, where from early Georgian days timber, glass, stone, coal and other materials were brought up the Avon from Bristol. It has its tradition as a cloth trade centre, since the days of Chaucer's Wyf of Bath:

> Of cloth making sche hadde such an haunt
> Sche passed hem of Ypris and of Gaunt.

It has its festival, its many flourishing societies promoting music, literature and the arts; it has its American museum, in a Regency mansion designed by Sir Jeffry Wyatville. But it has, pre-eminently, quite apart from its therapeutic fame, the ever-present aura of a town free from its inception or cured of all urban cramps, constrictions, nervous instability and other symptoms of planner's general paralysis. May this not be lost in the creeping tide of 'packing-case architecture', nor annulled by the effects of a new four-lane carriageway designed to tunnel under the heart of the Georgian area, euphemistically called the 'inner relief road'.

Chapter Three

EIGHTEENTH-CENTURY IMITATORS

'One would think the English were ducks! they are for ever waddling to the waters.' Horace Walpole's remark about a people called in Italy 'il populo dei cinque pasti' (the five-meal people) has peculiar relevance for that age of gluttony, the eighteenth century. It is conspicuous that the growth of wealth, comfort and leisure and the growth of hypochondria go together. Wealth, comfort and high living were on a continuous upward trend in England after the victories of Queen Anne's reign, the period of comparative peace abroad during the reigns of George I and George II and under Robert Walpole's successful administration. Those who chiefly took part in the exodus to the watering places were the aristocracy and upper-middle classes, who often ate and drank to excess and who could afford to compete with the company of their equals or betters in the social round. Under their patronage, as appears, what started as a cure for over-indulgence of one sort, soon became another sort of indulgence. The English urge to pursue pleasure in the form of duty (to one's health), to do one thing while calling it another, was gratified.

The development of Buxton as a resort was mainly due to the fifth Duke of Devonshire and his two successors. It had had its Roman patronage for the thermal 'milk-warm' springs: the nearby Bakewell, in whose parish the village of Buxton long remained, had baths and mild chaly-

beate waters which were used in Saxon times, and during the Plan-
tagenet and Tudor period Buxton itself was frequented by sufferers
from rheumatism. A treatise by a certain Dr Jones of Derby, in 1572,
testified to the springs' curative properties. Prior to the Reformation
the springs with their medical properties had been dedicated to St Ann,
mother of the Virgin, the saint who gives health and life to her devotees
and hope to the barren. Mary Queen of Scots visited Buxton on several
occasions to seek a cure for the rheumatism brought on by her im-
prisonment in cold, damp cells. Under Henry VIII's Vicar-General,
Thomas Cromwell, the use of these waters was prohibited at St Ann's
chapel and the crutches left by cured cripples were destroyed; but the
ban on and closure of the baths lasted only a comparatively short time.
A charity, known as 'The Treasury of the Bath', was set up to aid poor
people coming for treatment, many of whom derived 'unspeakable
benefit'. The water, bright, clear, tasteless and odourless, issuing from
limestone rocks between 3,500 and 5,000 feet below ground, continued
to be appreciated, although Buxton remained merely a village.

Buxton Hall, where the well and warm bath were located, belonged
to the Duke of Devonshire. The bath, at the end of the seventeenth
century, was of considerable size and substance—about 40 feet long and
20 or 30 feet broad. 'There is ten or twelve Springs that bubble up that
are a little warm—it is not so warm as milk from the cow [actually the
water is 82°F]—and not so quick a spring so that it is not capable of being
cleansed after everybody has been in. About ten or twelve yards distant
is a spring called St Ann's Well which is for drinking . . . the taste is not
unpleasant but rather like milk, they say it is Diuretick' (Celia Fiennes).
In 1780–4, at the direction of the fifth Duke of Devonshire, the
principal architectural feature of Buxton, the Crescent, was erected on
the actual site of the Roman baths, and the hub of an elegant town
centre was thus created. Its cost, according to report, was offset by one
year's revenue from his Grace's copper- and lead-mine properties in the
neighbourhood.

The architect of this sweeping, massive Palladian structure—it has a
curve of 200 feet, with wings extending a further 58 feet—was John
Carr, like John Wood, of Yorkshire origin. Based on Inigo Jones's
piazzas at Covent Garden, with their rusticated ground-floor arcades,

The Crescent and New Baths, Buxton

it has three storeys, of which the lowest forms a covered promenade, raised above the carriageway and reached by short flights of steps at intervals. The dining room, one of the most handsome in the kingdom, was decorated by Robert Adam. Carr (1703–1807), the son of a stone mason at Horbury, near Wakefield, became mayor of York: his fine classical work included the York Assize Courts and Gaol, the original designs for Harewood House (whose interior was remodelled by Adam), the model village and two elegant pavilions there, and Denton Park and Farnley Hall. He also designed the handsome grandstand, built in 1776, at Doncaster racecourse and the perfect mid-Georgian Constable Burton Hall. The Crescent had St Ann's Well in front of it, the Natural Baths (on the site of a Roman bath) at the western end and the Hot Baths in the eastern wing. Other attractive though more modest buildings were erected and grouped around it. Buxton as a resort was further laid in his Grace's debt by the Great Stables with their remarkable 150 feet wide unsupported dome (later becoming the Devonshire Royal Hospital) and the Duke's drive, a fine carriage road (1795). The circuit of the drive linking the Bakewell Road with the Ashbourne Road via Lover's Leap is about three miles and was much favoured by later visitors using pony carriages and bath chairs. With its Crescent and Quadrant, colonnade of shops and Broad Walk, its Pump Room and fine church in the Tuscan order, built in 1811 (and with later a vast Palace Hotel, an opera house and pavilion built, 1871, in iron and glass and described as a 'miniature Crystal Palace' and a Park laid out by Sir Joseph Paxton), Buxton soon came to possess all the expected features of a first-class watering place. Its water—closely resembling in composition that of Plombières—and its douche massage baths won a European repute. It possessed also something that was less expected and different in its situation: an elevation of almost 1,100 feet above sea-level gave it a tonic climate. The eighteenth-century comment on this situation as 'inhospitable to mankind, indulgent to wolves and beasts of prey' was changed by nineteenth-century promoters into 'the most bracing spa in the kingdom' or the 'mountain spa' as it could be called with a little imagination; but, to give assurance to nervous invalids, 'the covered ways in the town enable a walk to be taken in fresh air whatever the weather'. Another feature of the situation also came into its own. On his journey northwards in 1771 Boswell took the post-chaise from a very good inn, The Green Man at Ashbourne, the proprietress of which, 'a mighty civil gentlewoman', presented him with an engraving of the sign of her house and a 'short address' in the hope that he would name it to his extensive acquaintance. He thought this worth posting up in his journal, but passed through Buxton apparently without comment. In the same year Tabitha Bramble (*Humphry Clinker*) mentioned that in passing among the 'pearls of land and water' she had seen the 'Devil's-Harse a-pike' and 'Hoyden's Hole' near Buxton as the only noteworthy sights. Some fifty years or so later, however, Byron was enthusiastically declaiming that there were prospects in Derbyshire as noble as any in Greece or Switzerland. The development and popularisation of a taste for the picturesque (see Chapter Eight) was to have a considerable effect on the inland resort. On the advantage of its surrounding scenery Buxton based a good deal of its subsequent successful appeal. Hotels with an elevated situation, while advertising their southwestern aspect, proximity to baths, pavilion, gardens and Serpentine Woods by the Wye or their own velvety bowling greens, stressed also the 'romantic scenery of the Peak', the beauties of Dovedale, and the combination of superb setting and invigorating mountain air.

Here, in following the well-worn footpaths to the contrasting beauty of the limestone valleys—the glens, clefts and dingles which Ruskin lavishly praised as 'so narrow and precipitous, so winding and landlocked that they seem to possess their own sky'—the 'traveller finds his joy', the botanist and conchologist their treasures, and the seeker after health his stimulus and exercise. Prehistoric caverns, picturesque towers, 'Solomon's Temple' and old bridges diversify the interest of the cataracts, the sylvan or sombre valleys and cloughs. If visitors went further afield to trace associations among the surrounding villages, a pleasant minor feature to be noticed were the guide plates and the (continued) use of neat, antique-styled road signs with their distinctive lettering. It was the age of reading, for which many visitors found plenty of time. Boarding houses had large libraries, of which a few here and there survive; they took names like 'Pendennis' and could expect their inmates to be enthusiastic about *Peveril of the Peak*, *The Compleat Angler*, *Adam Bede* and many romances with local associations.

The layout of Buxton affords its own contrasts. Lower Buxton, the town of hotels and amusements, baths and hydros, is a centre of slightly monumental formality. From St Ann's Hotel, which occupies half of Carr's stately curve, one looks out on much the same scene as Queen Victoria saw when she stayed at the hotel in the other half, called The Crescent. The dignified, if not grandiose architecture and green spaciousness come as a surprise, especially when compared with that of other stone-built towns in the northern tradition just on the other side of the Peak. The leisurely atmosphere of cafes and gardens and covered shopping ways offers strong contrast to the normal workaday town; yet there is a family likeness in the rather sombre solidity and the leafiness of darker green about it all. Vera Brittain evoked its pre-1914 social life in her second novel, *Not Without Honour*.

Higher Buxton—the old village, less than 100 feet higher—has its market square and administrative buildings and cattle market, recalling the fact that Buxton claims, along with Alston, Cumberland, to be the highest market town in England and, in fact, enjoys the bustle of an open-air market each Saturday. The two, upper town and lower, are linked by St Ann's Cliff, which commands a bird's-eye view of Buxton and was laid out as a popular 'lounge', with flower beds, sloping lawns, terrace walks and bandstand. The 'Slopes' run gently down to the Pump Room, now used as an Information Centre.

Here then is central England's Harrogate—or second Bath—with its own distinctive speciality: the Well-dressing Festival at the peak of the season. (The birth-place of well-dressing is Tissington, near Ashbourne, where it commenced not later than 1615—the year of the great drought.) Like Harrogate, Buxton now leans a good deal on shopping facilities, coach tours, trade fairs, an annual antiques fair, exhibitions and business conferences as a resort, and as support for its hotels' bread and butter. If current road plans for the removal of all traffic from Spring Gardens, one of the two main shopping streets which leads to the Quadrant and Crescent, are fulfilled, Buxton will have its fashionable 'precinct' and be in less danger of 'running to seed' as once seemed to be possible. No traffic at present can pass along Broad Walk and this does much to recommend the quietness of certain hotels, with their outlook over pavilion gardens and lake. Buxton has two additional advantages—its position as gateway to Britain's first National Park 'The Peak', the 'roof of England' and, one of longer standing, as a winter sports centre in its own right. Where else in England could visitors who come to stroll in the summer season and drink the waters or watch county cricket return in winter for properly organised curling, ski-ing and Swiss-style tobogganing?

Bath, with a population of over 80,000, is about twice the size of Tunbridge Wells: Tunbridge is about twice that of Buxton (pop. 20,100): with the Malverns—Great Malvern, Malvern Wells, Little Malvern, Malvern West, North Malvern, South Malvern and Malvern Link taken together, a population can be reckoned approaching that of Tunbridge Wells. The site of the Holy Well which made the whole constellation's fame is in a suburb of Great Malvern and the magnitude of that star was itself, until early Victorian times, that of a village with some sixty houses. It contained a few clusters of thatched cottages, some scattered villas, a library-cum-stationery-cum-chemist's shop, a forge, four small hotels—one a seventeenth-century coaching inn, another of Regency date—a Pump Room and Baths (built 1819-23) and the old Priory. Comparisons therefore with Buxton, so far as architectural development goes, are out of court: but as a place of resort for those who sought cures, especially from scrofulous or eruptive complaints, it is no less strongly rooted in the eighteenth century and earlier times.

The Holy Well, above Malvern Wells, and St Ann's Well at Great Malvern both rise on the eastern side of a range of hills running north and south, composed of broken rocks of old date, and provide water of remarkable purity. (At its southern extremity the same belt of folded rock passes under the city of Bath and is met there by the folded and fractured rock of the Mendip system: where these two lines of disturbance cross, the Bath waters are enabled to rise through the earth's crust from the heated volcanic zone beneath.) For a cure of sore eyes 'people in troopes' resorted to the Malvern waters in the first half of the seventeenth century and baths in them were in special request for skin diseases. The water was bottled also at this period and sent as far afield as Berwick and London, to the tune of 1,000 bottles a week. Evelyn noted the healing of many infirmities, including sore eyes, leprosy and

Page 51 (*above*) An engraving of Bath; (*below*) an engraving of Matlock Bath

Page 52 (*above*) Municipal offices, Neptune fountain and statue of Dr Wilson in Cheltenham; (*below*) Cheltenham's classic Promenade

king's evil by the agency of the holy wells 'trickling out of a valley, thro a steep declivity towards the foot of the Great Malvern Hills'. The *Gazetteer* of 1738 mentions the Holy Well's efficacy in clearing the skin from sun-burnings and freckles and adding 'as much Lustre as agrees with concealed Art and Modesty'. The fashionable impulse, however, towards use of the waters, which led to Malvern's development as a spa, was to come from the publication on their properties issued by an eighteenth-century Worcester physician. Dr John Wall—celebrated founder of the Worcester porcelain manufactory—subjected samples to scientific analysis in order to determine their curative value and its cause. The book, published in 1756, dealt with the remarkable cures of ulcers, palsy, incipient blindness and other complaints effected by use of these waters in the past, and quickly ran into several editions. The Malvern waters were found to have nothing disagreeable, evil-smelling or foul-tasting about them—a distinction from those of many continental spas—and to be so pure and free from salts or mineral spirit that they could pass through the smallest absorbing vessels to enter the body. So, whether for bathing or lotion, they were nonpareil: a name was created and custom followed.

Between the 1750s and Dr Wall's retirement from practice in Malvern in 1774 came the beginning of the transformation of the Wells into a popular resort, with assembly balls, lotteries, public breakfasts and lodging accommodation. The first guide for visitors was brought out in 1796. Appropriately, Dr Wall retired to Bath, and his death is commemorated there by one of the 614 tablets on the walls of the abbey.

Patronage of the wells continued with some diminution for a time after Dr Wall's departure. It was sufficient for hotels to be built to supplement the lodging houses. One, Mount Pleasant, has an orangery. Another, the Foley Arms, built in 1810, was designed by the architects Samuel and John Deykes, who were also responsible for the Pump Room of 1819 and the Royal Library. The hotel still has its splendid cast-iron verandahs intact and also much of the original furnishing. The Pump Room's three-bay centre, with Doric columns, flanking entrance bays and a wreathed frieze formed a good stuccoed group in central Malvern along with the library's bow with columns and the Foley Arms, to which wings were added in the same decade. Visitors were thus encouraged—still more so when Princess Victoria and her mother spent some time at the resort in 1829, riding donkeys up to the foothills of the Malvern Hills. (Donkeys for hire for the less vigorous or elderly were almost as much a feature of the hillier resorts in the nineteenth century as they were for children's rides at the seaside.)

The real impetus to Malvern's growth, however, around this centre and a number of Regency houses in the adjoining Graham Road and Church Street, came in 1842 with the commercial exploitation of its water cure. Two doctors, James Wilson and James Manby Gully, the former an ex-pupil and patient of Vincenz Priessnitz, pioneer of hydropathy at Graefenberg, came to one of the hotels to prospect a place suitable for development as a spa. Dr Wilson acquired the lease of the hotel, which he named Graefenberg House, and started in hydropathic practice. Dr Gully soon afterwards built separate establishments, Tudor House and Holyrood House, for men and for women. His book *The Water Cure in Chronic Disease* ran into twelve editions between 1846 and 1874. Patients began to flow, even to flood in.

Their methods, though more sophisticated than Dr Wall's, under whom 'the usual practice in cutaneous foulness was to go into the water with the linen on, and dress upon it wet', were not dissimilar. The 'cure' was strict, combining hydropathic processes such as that just described or the douche—ice-cold water forcefully discharged from a pipe over the naked patient for a minute or more—with extraordinary intake of water, as much as thirty Graefenberg flasks full (about twelve tumblers), before breakfast, a meagre diet and exercise on the hills. As a regimen, pure water inside and out, fresh air and regular exercise could hardly do harm, nor could those who persisted with it fail to feel some beneficial effect. The fees, however, for this exposure to natural remedies were remarkably high.

Different spas promulgated different ideas about water drinking, dependent, of course, on the patient's complaint and the water's mineral content. 'Some imagine that the amount of benefit to be gained will depend on the quantity of water swallowed, or on the frequency with which doses are administered . . . In few cases ought a larger quantity than the contents of four pint tumblers be drunk each day, and these ought to be drunk early in the morning while the heat is less oppressive, the body and mind are refreshed by sleep and the stomach is empty . . . For the sake of the gas mineral water should always be drunk deliberately and with an interval of at least a quarter of an hour between each tumbler. Gentle walking exercise should follow the drinking of the waters.' The invalid, according to Dr Augustus Bozzi Granville, author of *Spas of England* and *Spas of Germany*, a thorough investigator and assessor of medicinal waters, should not only be careful in making use of the spa, but strictly attentive to his general habits. He should clean his teeth first with a brush and some proper tincture, burnt bread or sage leaves: take breakfast an hour after the last glass of water and then only one or two cups of coffee, milk or chocolate, and white bread without butter. He should fatigue neither his body nor his mind —but not sleep—before dinner, which ought to be easily digested and moderately nourishing. A light beer with plenty of hops, no porter or double beer to go with it: wine, as heating, not to be recommended. Supper time, eight o'clock, should again be an occasion of great moderation. Then, providing that the climate was suitable—not subject to gales of wind, lowering clouds, frequent showers, or marked variations in temperature—the waters might be efficacious and dyspepsy, for example, set at bay. It was stressed that only functional derangements, not organic complaints, could be so treated.

To the six wells already discovered, the Royal Malvern at West Malvern was added in the Queen's reign. St Ann's was the most popular in public use, being nearest to the town and very agreeable to the taste, extremely light and cold (48° F). A mineral water factory was established at Holy Well. From another well in private hands water sold at a shilling a gallon and was sent off by coach and carrier. In the heyday of their popularity in the mid-nineteenth century, one might see the 'Cold Waterers' walking from one spring to another, drinking in measured sips from each and from the numerous rills on the roadside. Coaches and flies went past every ten minutes. Dickens, Macaulay, Darwin and Bulwer Lytton were among the distinguished visitors. In 1850 Dickens's wife was recuperating at Malvern with 'Georgy' (Georgina Hogarth) for company: his farce in association with Mark Lemon, *Mr Nightingale's Diary*, is set in Malvern Wells and includes a 'malade imaginaire'. Macaulay took a villa for August and September 1851. Lytton's experience of the regime's severity—he was compelled to abandon some rich pastries he had just bought when Dr Wilson met him in the street and spotted them—did not detract from his glowing praise of an autumn cure. As many as seventy-four different techniques of bathing and friction treatment were recommended by one practitioner. One might compare this patronage of the latest fashionable pick-me-up with that, reported in the *Radio Times*, in August 1971, of a male star spending a week at a Bedfordshire 'health farm' for sauna baths and friction rubs, before starting his month's holiday. In Malvern itself one of the hydros has 're-entered the health business' recently under the direction of a TV personality, for 'toning up, weight reduction or pure relaxation'.

As a watering place—'the metropolis of the water-cure'—Malvern Spa flourished exceedingly, especially after the railway came, for as long as its specialists pumped up enthusiasm, and their own profits. Dr Wilson's death in 1867, Dr Gully's departure, and the death of another colleague Dr Grindrod, specialist in lung diseases and compressed air chamber therapy, all occurring within a few years, took away a certain dynamism essential to popularity. Malvern remained a resort, but for other than the original reasons. A hotel advertisement in the nineties, for Dr Fergusson's Hydropathic Establishment and winter residence at Great Malvern, 'the garden of England', stressed this. It claimed to be a delightful residence for patients, visitors, rest and change, 500 feet above the sea, with dry, bracing, sunny conditions, the purest of water, gravelly soil and a sheltered position. There was tennis, bowls, croquet, golf, billiards and hunting as well as massage, douches, plunge swimming baths and 'perfect sanitary arrangements'. And, perhaps by way of assurance to those who had heard of the spartan rigours of the Malvern cure, an excellent cuisine coupled with the guarantee of 'patients receiving every kindness and attention'. The attractiveness of the district, the equable climate and dry clear air, the lonely hills enjoyable for their own sake—hills from which William Langland had received the 'Vision of Piers Plowman'—all contributed to Malvern's image. It was, like Bath and Cheltenham, popular with retired colonial servants and army officers; it was visited, in 1891, by Princess Mary of

Teck and members of the German court; its terraced hillside site, above the old Priory, gave it something of a continental flavour. It was found that weariness and anaemia, fret and worry, could soon be thrown off in an air as delightful as that of the Engadine, with facilities for exercise on the breezy 'mountain' sides increased by nine miles of smooth firm carriage roads in approach. As in the past celebrities like Elizabeth Barrett Browning and Jenny Lind had lived there, so to praise residence later there were Shaw, Elgar, Stanley Baldwin.

The views from Malvern—taking in the cathedrals of Worcester, Gloucester, Hereford, the Welsh hills, the Severn valley and, on a perfect day, a prospect of fifteen counties—are engrossing in their variety and chequerboard colours. With a lower mean daily range of temperature than either Buxton, Cheltenham or Tunbridge Wells, Malvern is specially favoured for winter as well as summer stays. It claims both low rainfall and an enviable freedom from fog—in short an ideal place for either residence or retirement, or for healthy schooling. 'Balcony commanding magnificent views', 'excellent winter home', 'heated throughout', 'three minutes public garden, churches, and golf links', began to appear on the hotel brochures. 'We can hardly say more than that the prospect (from an upper room in the Foley Arms) struck us as far finer than from the terrace over the Thames at Richmond.' (The same, I found, could be well said of that from the Mount Pleasant grounds.)

So as the vogue of the spa lost ground (though the cold water, the purest in Britain, continued to gush from the hard volcanic syenite) these merits kept Malvern alive as a health and pleasure centre. At the 1921 census the estimated visiting population, 25,000, exceeded the resident population. The town is itself an enjoyable period-piece, largely Victorian of course. There is Wilson's later establishment in Abbey Road, with giant pilasters and a Greek Doric porch, Italianate stuccoed villas of the forties with round-arched window lights, the long terraces of Lansdowne Crescent and Foley Terrace with its fiftyish tower, barge-boarded Tudor villas, Jacobean brick ones and some ambitious Gothic mansions. With its buildings climbing dramatically up the hills, its conspicuous and amusing roof features—domes, belfries, spires, turrets and belvederes on the Gothic piles—its central Priory grounds and Winter Gardens, its Gothic revival churches, its gabled, long and low railway station and nearby Imperial Hotel (eminently Gothic, 1861–2, purchased later for the Girls' College), there is ample interest for a perambulation. One can still detect the faint painted signs of old hotels which have been converted into shops, and see in prep. schools their lodging house origins, or in bank and business premises the sites of former library and pump-room buildings.

Malvern's favourable position and unspoiled environment has attracted to the district five independent girls' boarding schools since the end of last century, in addition to Malvern College (a boys' public school, erected 1863–5 to cater for the sons of Army officers and Indian civil servants who had retired there), which absorbed Dr Grindrod's hydro. The successful foundation of the Ladies' College at Cheltenham, in the fifties, had early demonstrated the advantages of establishing a school at a spa town. These establishments bring their periodical influx of youth to the town—and youth's parents to the hotels, to mingle perhaps with socialising businessmen from Worcester and Birmingham, who use it as a dormitory town. Malvern is also the home of radar: the Royal Radar Establishment, which arrived in great secrecy during World War II, has both brought a new impetus and added to the youthful outlook.

A noteworthy addition to the cultural attractions and cynosure to music-lovers is Malvern's association with Edward Elgar, who in younger days built up a teaching practice among the schools and from his house 'Forli' in Alexandra Road produced some of his finest early work. Elgar's passion for kite-flying and walking was indulged on the same Malvern Hills that inspired his cantata *Caractacus*: and friends he made at this period figured in the *Enigma Variations*. When the Malvern Festival was inaugurated in 1929 by Sir Barry Jackson, founder of Birmingham Repertory Company, 'to unite the characteristics of a garden-party, a picnic and a healthy summer holiday with investigation into modern drama', the town was put on the map dramatically as well as musically for a wider public than either Dr Wall or Dr Wilson could ever have envisaged. To the Festival, and equally to the annual Three Counties Agricultural Show at Malvern Wells, the perennial 'Englishness' of the setting provides a special background appeal. Malvern is perhaps less grand than its repute, but no one can approach the Malvern Hills without feeling a lift of the spirits.

Chapter Four

REGENCY RIVALS

LEAMINGTON, another doctors' town, came to Camden's notice as he compiled the first topographical survey of England (published in Latin in 1586) on account of its natural saline waters. His perceptive comments on the conditions of places in his day led him to add this note to another 'mineral water or spaw' deeply impregnated with iron and vitriol minerals, in the grounds of the Earl of Derby, near Lathom Park, Lancashire: 'The want of convenient lodging and other accommodations, make it less frequented, but 'tis certain it has done some notable cures, one particularly which an ingenious Gentleman affirms to have been one of the greatest and quickest that he ever knew done by any such water.' The want of convenient lodging and accommodation was no doubt partly the cause of Leamington's comparatively late development as a spa. Two hundred years after Camden's notice, and after both Speed and Dugdale had commented on its springs of salt water 'much used by the inhabitants for seasoning their meat', its population was under 300—only six of them being entitled to vote. The well on waste land south of the river Leam, where the original hamlet (Lamintone in *Domesday*) belonged, was open for use by the poor: its chief virtue was supposed to be the cure of hydrophobia. Change began when Dr Holyoake, a Warwick physician, in 1784 offered the land-owner, Lord Aylesford, the sum of one thousand pounds for a building lease of the site. Its potentialities were recognised. The offer was declined lest the poor be kept out, but development of the town soon began.

By 1820 the population of Leamington had moved up from 315 to
over 2,000, although as late as 1808 the actor Macready recorded that it
was only a small village of thatched houses, not one tiled or slated, with
only one modest inn. The layout, on the northern side, of Union and
Upper Union Parade (now The Parade) and of Cross Street (now
Regent Street) began the process of turning the village into a town. A
long terrace on the curve, the start of the Parade in 1815, has giant
coupled pilasters opposite the Greek Doric porches of Euston Place.

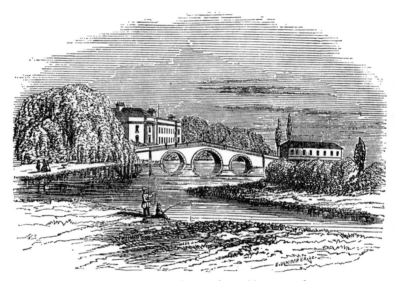

Leamington, from Dr Thomson's *Health Resorts of Britain*

The fifth Earl of Aylesford erected the housing of the original well, in
1813, and the first Pump Room, designed by C. S. Smith with a Tuscan
colonnade, was put up by a small syndicate over a copious spring discovered in 1808. A special wing was set aside for free use by the poor
on two days each week. Four years later the building of a hotel on the
Parade, regarded in that day as the largest in Europe, was completed
and by the Prince Regent's command—he came over from Warwick
Castle to see the opening—became the Regent's Hotel. Visits by
Princess Augusta, the Crown Prince and Princess of Denmark, the
Duke and Duchess of Gloucester and other notabilities followed.

Assembly Rooms, originally 'The Parthenon', with a fine Corinthian portico, were erected in Bath Street in 1821. The spa was well and truly established.

The 'new town' on the northern side of the river was completely unlighted up to the early twenties, until gas could be imported from a new company formed at Warwick and eighteen lamp standards set up on the Parade. (Warwick for a time considerably benefited in general trade by the development of Leamington, since many people came to buy in Warwick shops before good shops had been built at the Spa.) From this time until about 1840 was the golden period for the town's architectural development. Warwick Street, crossing the Parade, the Clarendon Hotel, with its giant pilasters and Doric porches, Beauchamp Square, Clarendon Square, Portland Street with its classical villas and, beyond the line of the Parade, Binswood Avenue belong to this period. No less important for the town's appearance and development was the opening up of an estate, Newbold Comyn, bequeathed by the Reverend Edward Willes (who died in December 1820) to his philanthropically disposed son. A road was cut through the estate, from Holly Walk (where in *Dombey and Son* Dickens was to set the scene for Carker's first meeting with Edith Granger) to the Parade; room was left for terraces, squares and crescents, but Newbold Meadows were preserved from the builder and presented to the town. With garden-flanked Newbold Terrace and Regent Grove and Hamilton Terrace facing into a central tree-lined walk after the French manner, the style was set for the spacious dignity of the greater part of the town centre. All Saints' Church, in the French Gothic style, on which building commenced in 1843, was to be one of the largest parish churches in the kingdom. The wideness of the streets and breathing spaces in its midst combined to make it one of the most desirable health resorts in the country.

Leamington as a rising spa was fortunate that its period of growth coincided with one of the soundest eras of British architecture. In complementary style to the beautiful sweep of the Lower Parade, the fine curve of Lansdowne Crescent, the elegant pairs of cottages (by W. Thomas) of Lansdowne Circus in one of which, No 10, Nathaniel Hawthorne lived, and the classical simplicity of Clarendon Square, where Napoleon III resided for a time after 1870, many individual Regency houses, less formally disposed, have lines which have led critics to find in Leamington's villas 'her peculiar glory'. They were designed to fit in with their neighbours and with regard to trees and grass, a relationship which has helped greatly to determine the character of a town intended to harmonise with gracious rural surroundings. Most buildings undertaken by Regency architects were faced with stucco, unless there was a plentiful local supply of suitable stone. This durable cement—common to the classical terraces of Regent's Park and Brighton—was originally painted to resemble Bath stone, but nowadays is painted white or cream. It sets off admirably the delicate ornamental ironwork, in Grecian balconies, railings, verandahs and porches which so much enhance the Spa's appearance—though they are not in such profusion or variety of design as at Cheltenham.

When Sophia Wilson, sister of the notorious Harriette, Regency courtesan of scandalous memoirs, married Lord Berwick, it may be recalled that she withdrew 'to propriety and Leamington Spa'. The place certainly would seem to offer an antidote to the raffish—despite the Brightonesque terraces: its repute, indeed, was medical, its equable temperature and dry climate especially favouring the invalid. It attracted, among others of the famous, Longfellow, Sarah Bernhardt and the Duke of Wellington. In tribute to the mainstay of its high medical reputation, Dr Henry Jephson, a brilliant physician, who received Queen Victoria in 1838 and contributed much to the planning of the town, the meadows which came to the community under the dispensation of Edward Willes were called 'Jephson Gardens'. They contain a memorial obelisk to Willes, an eight-column Corinthian temple housing a statue to the doctor (one of whose appreciative patients was Ruskin), and a terracotta fountain to another medical benefactor, Dr Hitchman. The town became Royal Leamington Spa by the Queen's grant: the gardens with the large lake, in which two fountains play (exact replicas of those at Hampton Court), their shaded arbours, their maze and lavish flowerbeds have still a discernible Victorian atmosphere. One half expects the leisurely promenaders to be dressed in frock coats and crinolines as they admire the 'carpet bedding' or drift towards the aviary. Archery and croquet, open air

Shakespearean performances and illuminated promenade concerts used to be their summer attractions. Quiet, restful, even languorous beside the slow-flowing Leam, the gardens face the Royal Pump Room, which has its own pleasure grounds for fetes, folk dancing and trampoline. With Victoria Park just beyond, along Archery Road, they seem to muffle the southern approaches to the town against too strident modernity.

The spa grew rapidly, to 13,000 by 1846, and the railway coming a couple of years earlier enabled travellers from London to reach Leamington in four and a half hours. But before the end of that decade the fashion for taking the waters had already begun its decline and the Pump Rooms were no longer the handsomely paying propositions that they had been. After the original syndicate had sold out the new owner himself, in 1860, felt compelled to advertise their closure and his intention to put them up for sale for building use. At that point local patriotism, fanned by the Leamington Spa *Courier*, came into play. A new company was formed, improvements were carried out including the addition of a pediment to the facade (since removed), the local Board of Health shortly took over and the town was able to retain the feature on which its early fortunes were centred.

A useful fillip, and a foresign of future interests for Leamington, was the founding in 1872 of the world's first lawn tennis club there. *The Handbook to Croquet*, one of Routledge's early 'Yellow Backs', had already taken Leamington as an example of an 'in' town devoted to that once-popular sport.

Queen Victoria in much larger-than-life marble replica, before the red brick and brown stone campanile of the Renaissance-style Town Hall, looks out on a Parade which has still the unspoiled and inviting sweep of her times, especially now that the electric trams are no more. Doric columns and porches, giant pilasters, highly decorated iron balconies and railings are details which arrest the eye even where the stylish shop-fronts clamour for sole attention. In spring and early summer the tree-lined avenues—elms, planes, lindens—add their distinctive town-in-the-country air, although the population which had already gone up to 21,000 by 1875 has more than doubled since that time. The central features of 'leafy Leamington', especially its Regency buildings, have wherever possible been preserved amid new developments, of which the more recent are high blocks of flats. Many American visitors since Hawthorne's day have responded to the regularity, width and whiteness of streets which recall their own best examples. (Recent population increases have come from immigration rather than birthrate within the town, which has the lower birthrate yet high proportion of females to males, that are the normal phenomena of spa towns, so often chosen for residence in middle life. The fact that it is primarily a residential, recreational spa community—although the setting up of a arge Lockheed factory to employ some thousands indicates a possible new bias in the future—gives Leamington both status and confidence: along with Kenilworth and Warwick it forms a population unit large enough to be self-sufficient.)

Four aspects of the resort continue to draw visitors. First its accessibility and position as a Midland shopping centre, for things other than daily needs. Then its convenience as a gateway to the Shakespeare country. Again its special sports connexions; as it began with lawn tennis and encouraged cycling (with a good track in Victoria Park), so it has gone on to provide the venue for open bowls tournaments, for an International Fencing Tournament, annual archery tournaments and for AAA events. Finally, but by no means to be relegated to last in importance, it has its saline waters of the muriated sulphine variety, in apparently inexhaustible supply from the marls and red sandstone upon which the town is built.

Each year many thousands of patients attend the Royal Pump Room for a wide range of treatment under physiotherapists and hydrotherapists or to drink the waters served from the Fountain. Leamington, Bath, Droitwich, Woodhall Spa and, recently again, Cheltenham, are the only five English spas still in business. Those who take morning coffee or afternoon tea, to the music of the Spa orchestra, in the dignified Pump Room restaurant and then stroll forth into the peaceful gardens just across the road, enter a kind of oasis, where time might have stood still since Dr Jephson's day. One of the hotels used to advertise itself as sloping to the river Leam, facing the Pump Room gardens and in close proximity to both railway stations 'thus making it one of the prettiest places of resort in the Kingdom'. One could agree with the dictum, if not with all the definitives of its expression.

'The new Arizona of England, Britain's garden of rest, the proud, but prim place of refuge from all the squabbles and squalls, from the strumming and yelling: the stronghold of old-fashioned Englishness'—the West Country, with its ranks of ex-colonials hugging the sun in Sidmouth, Budleigh Salterton and Cheltenham Spa, has been so defined. The history of Cheltenham as a stronghold of old-fashioned English-ness begins somewhat earlier than that of Leamington: its saline springs first became known in 1715, and its architectural budding began shortly afterwards. But there is no question about its popularity depending on liver trouble contracted in the East. A situation open to the mild airs of the Severn plain, while protected on north and east by a steep limestone escarpment, gives Cheltenham the moderate winter, gentle spring and almost languorous summer especially favoured by retired Anglo-Indians seeking the waters. Fresh from Simla and Poona—places themselves built to resemble the glories of Chelten-ham—they found and preserved there some of the spaciousness and graciousness of life to which, as a ruling caste, they were accustomed.

In the seventeenth century Cheltenham, like Winchcombe, Glouces-tershire, was a tobacco town, one of the first places in England to grow tobacco: its chief concern was farming and its buildings were of brick and thatch. Government prohibition of plantations and the cheapness of Virginian tobacco killed this trade: the malt trade became its main support and Cheltenham seemed likely to continue as a small market town, with the usual corn and butter market on stone pillars in the High Street. Discovery of the medicinal springs completely changed the pattern (though Dickens in *Nicholas Nickleby* still refers to a 'Cheltenham tobacconist').

The first spring, near the river Chelt, was given a well-house with a thatched roof and let for £61 per year. As more springs were dis-covered in other parts of the town, landowners, with the development of Bath in mind and keen business instincts for their own and the town's future, established several small 'spas' or 'spa-lets' with their separate buildings, the Pittville, Montpellier and Sherborne, chiefly in the area south of the old High Street. A retired Bristol sea-captain, whose wife

had inherited the original spring, was the first to plan a small resort—
such as Bristol Hotwell—with the support of his friends and some
wealthy patrons. A design for a long avenue, with a vista of the church
spire, to form a self-contained promenade for the water drinkers, and
a new layout for the old well-head materialised in 1738: Old Well
Walk rose up the lower slopes of Bayshill. The sea-captain's son and a
London associate built the first Long Rooms for the entertainment of
visitors, Dr Samuel Johnson, Handel and the Countess of Huntingdon

Cheltenham, from Dr Thomson's *Health Resorts of Britain*

among them. In 1786 the corn and butter markets were swept away to
allow for foot pavements to add to the visitors' comfort.

The summer visit of King George III, two years later, gave the town
its first taste of real distinction and augured well for the future, although
progress was still slow. His Majesty's health was proving a cause of
anxiety: his physician diagnosed gout and prescribed a regimen without
riding—which the king refused to give up—and the mildly purgative
waters of Cheltenham. He lodged in Bayshill, rising before dawn to
bustle down to the spa three hundred yards away in order to drink
three full bumpers. After taking a walk he drank more of the water:

such quantities had a violent effect and after trial and error he found a pint and a half to be the proper dose to give him 'two openings'. King George paid high tribute to the benefit of this salubrious spring, which cleared him without 'any sinking' or the least heating and without recourse to rhubarb pills. The Princess Royal took only half the dose, three-quarters of a pint, but the other Princess, Elizabeth, had to take rhubarb. While their stay lasted the King and Queen Charlotte dined at 4pm and in the evening walked on the walls or watched the lodge servants playing cricket. At Worcester, on their return journey, they visited a house that was being converted into a porcelain shop.

So far Cheltenham was basically a market town, with poor communications, trying to transform itself into a resort. Apart from paved walks it needed terraces of houses and hotels for visitors' accommodation; and for building materials for these it needed transport. A canal was planned, in 1792, but the Napoleonic wars—which incidentally helped to encourage the growth of English spas and bathing places by putting a temporary stop to foreign travel—prevented any large-scale developments then. The Gloucester and Cheltenham Rail and Tramway, 1811, provided the answer. It was extended by a branch to the stone quarries on Leckhampton Hill, south of the town. So, like Bath, Cheltenham had its building materials to hand. Individuals of vision and good taste were not lacking to envisage the possibilities of large-scale improvements and, with the help of eminent architects, to plan a resort equal to the first in England. The plans, brought to fruition within a comparatively short period, resulted in a homogeneous Regency town, a typical and elegant expression of its age. (The number of houses in Cheltenham, in 1811, was 1,556: in 1821, 2,411 and in 1831 about 5,000.)

New Assembly Rooms (now destroyed) in High Street were opened formally by the Duke of Wellington in 1816 and included one of the finest ballrooms in England. One of the early housing schemes, the Royal Crescent linked to Royal Well Road, would seem to acknowledge the builders' and architect's debt to the inspiration of Bath. Much of the town was laid out by J. B. Papworth (1775–1847), employed by Lord Sherborne, an architect well known for his books of rustic or

suburban villas with their aquatint plates. Between 1825 and 1830 his
Lansdowne Place, Montpellier Rotunda, shops in Montpellier Walk
and a number of villas enhanced by Ionic columns were going up. They
combine stylistic echoes with their own distinctive atmosphere: Montpellier Walk is further distinguished by replicas, between the shops, of
the Erechtheon caryatids in white stucco, the sculptor being Rossi. On
the north side John Forbes was responsible for the fine Ionic Pump
Room, 1825, on the Pittville estate, while G. A. Underwood, pupil of
Sir John Soane, designed Greek villas in the park, terraces to the south
of High Street and the Masonic Hall. There are seemingly endless terraces and villas in Cheltenham; the town is a veritable repository of
classical styles, where it is still possible to see Greek revival architecture
exactly as it looks in Ackermann.

Thomas Moore, a spa-goer who had journeyed on from Bath to
Leamington in August 1818, came to Cheltenham by coach from
Birmingham during the early development period. He visited a book-
seller, Mr Williams, enquired after a friend who was expected there
and was gratified to find a note at his hotel directed to 'the immortal
Thomas Moore Esq'. Communications, however, still left something to be desired: he found to his disappointment that no coach
left Cheltenham for Bath, about six hours' journey, on Sunday.
Another celebrated visitor, Lord Byron, first proposed marriage to
Miss Millbanke in the old Assembly Room—and married her in
1815.

The Queen's Hotel, 1838, at one end of the Promenade—Cheltenham's smartest street, immensely enhanced by the Regency terrace on
one side, whose height, length and architectural emphasis at centre and
wings give it scale and dignity—was designed by R. W. and C. Jearrad.
The building's bold stucco facade and decoration of coloured crowns,
with its row of Corinthian columns, said to be based on the Temple of
Jupiter, Rome, provides the street's striking terminus. R. W. Jearrad
also designed the romantic and impressive Christ Church (1837) whose
incredible pinnacled tower dominates the Malvern Road area. The
neighbourhood of the park combined elegant stucco villas in Greek and
Italian style with others in Tudor and Swiss, laid out by T. Billings, and
as new buildings continually appeared during the forties and fifties (the

number of houses by 1851 had reached 7,365) further pages were added
to the repository of styles. Many of the period terraces, such as those in
Imperial Square and St George's Road, were designed, like that on the
Promenade, as one imposing unit.

The rebuilding of the theatre, burned down in 1839, was prevented
for a time by the puritanical clergyman Dean Close, who laid the
foundation stone for Christ Church, and to whom drink, racing,
dramatic performances and Sunday trains were equally anathema. He
did however give Cheltenham its start as an educational centre.
Cheltenham Ladies' College was founded in 1853, originally as a day
school for the daughters of upper-middle-class residents: later it transferred to new buildings at Bayshill which shared in the bold Anglo-
Italian architectural manner. All in all spacious street planning, with
room for mature trees, fountains and broad pavements, attention to
detail apart from mere facade, clean stone and bright stucco give this
resort an originality and gaiety that sets it apart from Bath. Leaving
out the flame-of-the-forest trees and the coppersmith birds it might
well suggest to a later generation of colonial servants comparisons
with the sunny colonnades and gardens of Connaught Place, New
Delhi.

Another feature, belonging especially to the Regency town, was the
ornamental cast-ironwork on so many of the houses. Cheltenham was
fortunate in acquiring its balconies, railings, porches and verandahs to
set off the plain facades from foundries at the earliest stages of mass
production methods, when ironwork was at the peak of its quality.
The delicate designs, mostly from Cottingham's Smith and Founder
Directory, 1813, run into hundreds. They are usually on the Grecian
pattern: their curves, circles and half-circles, like climbing plants reduced to basic form or sometimes lace, afford a constant pleasure to the
eye especially when sunlight duplicates the design in shadow, on a
mellow stone or stucco wall. Some of the short streets lying back from
the High Street—itself now overtaken by steel and glass commercialism—offer a wealth of samples; there are others on the Promenade
terrace and in London Road. Suitably, and nearly always, the ironwork
is painted green.

An interesting sidelight concerning the roads and streets in English

IRSB—E

resorts is their mutual borrowing of names. Bath with its Royal
Crescent, Montpellier and Lansdowne; Leamington with Lansdowne
Crescent and Lansdowne Street and Ranelagh Terrace; Cheltenham
with its Royal Crescent, Lansdown Crescent, Place and Parade,
Montpellier Walk, Street, Terrace and Gardens, and Malvern Road;
Harrogate with Cheltenham Crescent, Mount and Parade, and Montpellier Parade; Great Malvern with Lansdowne Crescent; Llandrindod
with Montpellier Park; the many hotels and boarding houses with
other resorts' names; all reveal community of taste and interdependence
of ideas if not virtual interbreeding. The town of Montpellier, to take
a recurrent favourite, had a situation and climate which 'long procured
it great reputation as an asylum for persons whose delicate health
required a more temperate air than that of England'. 'The public walks
about Montpellier are superior to most in the beauty of their prospects,
owing to its elevated situation' (J. E. Smith; *Tour on the Continent*,
1793). Leamington more recently has acquired an enclave of roads
and avenues named after the picturesque resorts Coniston, Keswick,
and Windermere with Borrowdale Drive, Cockermouth Close,
Troutbeck Avenue, Ullswater Avenue, Wasdale Close and others in
support.

'What is so attractive about Cheltenham? I don't know, but it's a
lovely place: coming here is like stepping back fifty years.' The
response, though understandable, is not wholly in Cheltenham's
favour. Like Bath when the tide of fashion turned away from water-
drinking, Cheltenham became a favourite home for the leisured, the
retired, the ex-crown servants. The central spa, where four different
medicinal waters were dispensed, the Winter Gardens, the daily municipal concerts, were seen as survivals from another age. For prosperity
today the tradition of spacious street planning (which lasted up to 1914),
the leisurely promenade under the chestnuts, the cafe tables and striped
umbrellas spreading from Imperial Gardens to pavement, the forty
miles of avenues with their forty thousand trees and many flowering
varieties, the public schools and Pittville Pump Room restored to its
pristine splendour are not in themselves enough. In the space of a
generation, 1937–64, forty-two of the town's hotels had to close—a
measure of Cheltenham's decline as a seasonal resort. The late King's

physician, Lord Horder, could speak of it as a centre for the combination of health, rest, beauty and elegant entertainment—'those inestimable things which people need more and more'. But in 1963 the town council came out in favour of discontinuing the 'health and spa' myth of Cheltenham: it had already given up its medical baths and treatment centres.

The new image of Cheltenham as the holiday shopping centre of the West, halfway along the great trunk road from London to Wales, is mirrored in the fashion houses. Both Bond Street and Paris couture are well represented. The adoption of a continental system of disc parking, the first of its kind in this country, helps to encourage the customer. As a place of genteel retirement, the apparent changelessness of the town has its particular attraction; but though building speculators must still conform to Regency style, behind the scenes light engineering industries have steadily grown. Printing and aircraft accessory production, the making of watches, clocks and precision instruments, the manufacture of air-venting equipment and thermostatic valves, help to give substance and balance to Cheltenham's economy. The first successful turbo-jet aircraft was designed and assembled in a Cheltenham workshop; there is a first-class airport within four miles.

The municipal motto 'Salubritas et eruditio', based on the town's educational repute, is also being substantiated in contemporary style. Cheltenham culture offers a taste of town life, more metropolitan than provincial. The Opera House, transformed in appearance and renamed the Everyman Theatre, mounts productions of the highest standard, often putting on plays before their London opening. The concert room in the palatial town hall attracts world-famous vocalists, instrumentalists and conductors. The July Festival, started in 1945, has as its basic theme first performances of new works by British conductors; the November Festival is devoted to literature and involves established literary figures in talks and late night discussions. At the competitive Music Festival, held in May, new artistes have a chance of starting a successful career. Its wealth of antique shops, antiquarian bookshops, its gallery displays of paintings and porcelain, add further to the cultural enjoyment of Cheltenham residents and visitors. Nowadays a well-known Georgian hotel advertises itself as 'close to Town Hall, Promenade and shops, unofficial headquarters for lovers of the arts in Festival time'. None makes mention of proximity to the now self-service Pittville spa,⋆ but they suggest instead 'a perfect venue for touring the Cotswolds' and perhaps as make-weight 'parking free without lights'.

⋆ In 1968 the wells were polluted by a leak from oil used to fire the Pump Room's central heating and production stopped. New access has been made to the well and so the courtesy title 'spa', part of the image of gracious living and sophistication, is not subject to challenge under the Trade Descriptions Act.

Chapter Five

VICTORIAN DEVELOPMENTS

OF THE four watering places whose development into resorts was essentially Victorian—Droitwich, Harrogate, Ilkley and Matlock—the smallest, Droitwich, and the largest, Harrogate, are the strongest survivors as health centres today. Droitwich, an older town in origin in the centre of England, has stayed modest and compact with a population of about ten thousand: Harrogate has spread itself, claims that five hundred new families buy or build a house to reside there every year, and currently has a population of about sixty thousand. Ilkley and Matlock each have about twenty thousand. All had their period of development in the thirties, forties and fifties of the last century. Yet no one set down overnight in any one of these four would be at all likely to mistake it in the morning for any of the others.

Harrogate's first well, the chalybeate Tewit Well, was discovered in 1571 by William Slingsby who noted its resemblance to medicinal waters on the Continent. By calling it 'The English Spa' in 1596, Dr Timothy Bright brought that term into the language with its current usage. The 'Sulphur Spring' was mentioned by Dr Deane, and a medical treatise was written about its waters in 1626. The 'John Well' or 'Sweet Spaw', also chalybeate and, like Tewit, also in High Harrogate, was discovered in 1631, its medicinal qualities recognised by Dr Stanhope and the first building erected there in 1656. It was regarded as 'very good to wash eyes and pleasant to drink'. Four wells in Bogs

Field (subsequently 'Valley Gardens'), two being sulphur and two vitrioline, were mentioned by Dr John French in 1652.

The new spa's early fame rested on the old sulphur or 'stinking spaw'. According to Celia Fiennes, connoisseur of spaws at the end of the seventeenth century, it was a 'quick purger and good for all scurbetick humours', but had an offensiveness 'like carrion or a jakes'. (Some would say that it still has, after inspection of it in the basement of the Pump Room museum, and that it is still necessary 'to hold your breath so as to drink it down'.) All told, thirty-six springs, most of which are now revealed only by their iron bolted cases, camouflaged green among the lawns and flowerbeds of the Valley Gardens, were to be found in Low Harrogate; and each was of a different chemical composition. The outstanding feature of Harrogate as a spa was this diversity of the waters. In the early course of the nineteenth century, as more springs came to light in various places—the 'Cheltenham' chloride of iron spring was discovered in 1819, the 'Montpellier' sulphur, by the proprietor of a hotel, in 1822—the total reached eighty-eight within a radius of two miles. Those in High Harrogate enjoyed popularity first and a village grew up around them, patronised on a similar footing to Tunbridge; but the Sulphur Springs of Low Harrogate, found efficacious for gout, rheumatism and digestive ailments, as well as for skin diseases, gained ground and greater repute.

The earliest known engraving of 'Harrowgate Wells', showing four well-heads in a low-walled enclosure, was drawn in 1773 by Moses Griffiths, servant of Thomas Pennant of 'picturesque' repute. Laurence Sterne, the sentimental journeyer, was among those of the period who resorted to Harrogate. The notably captious traveller, Tobias Smollett, could not account for the concourse of people he found there 'upon any other principle than caprice, which seems to be the character of our nation'. Harrigate (*sic*) had a wild common, bare and bleak, paltry inns with cramped airless rooms, water like bilge-water and baths 'stinking like the pot of Acheron'. The lodges of each inn formed a distinct society that ate together: breakfast was in deshabille, there was tea-drinking in the afternoon, and cards or dancing in the evening in the way of dissipation. Young clothiers from Leeds came to cut a figure there—as they do today. When the diarist Silas Neville passed that way, in 1781, he observed a country somewhat like Newmarket Heath, a situation high and dry in a very keen air, 'which may contribute to the good effect of the waters'. The houses then available for the accommodation of the company looked more like gentlemen's seats than inns. A mezzotint by John Raphael Smith shows water drinkers at the St John Well, 1796, with a stone building. A structure of pillars and a canopy was erected in 1804 by public subscription over one of the sulphur well-heads. A Rowlandson drawing has the attendant 'nymph' at the Sulphur Well handing a tumbler to a Dr Syntax type of patron, while local gentry stand about in attitudes of fashionable languor. The Pump Room was still to be built. In short, while Harrogate lacked neither celebrity nor clientele before its nineteenth-century flowering, it lacked proper development.

On an 1821 map Harrogate still hardly exists as a town. There are small clusters of buildings in the vicinity of the Old Swan Hotel—one of those which looked 'more like gentlemen's seats'—and near the present White Hart; also close to Christ Church, where 'Paradise Row' is later to be transformed into Park Parade. A few modest late-Georgian houses and some Regency balconies are still to be seen here and in the adjoining Regent's Parade. In the more central West Park (formerly Prospect Row) a handsome terrace has been started with four houses having Tuscan or Ionic doorways or porches. The Granby Hotel, facing the Stray, belongs to this year but has later additions, including a four-column porch in the 1840s. Williams Bath, the first public bathing establishment (known later as Victoria Baths), was built in 1832; the Montpellier Baths were laid out in 1835 and in that year Cheltenham Spring got its classical Pump Room and Royal Promenade (from John Williams). Between them, in 1839, the Victoria and Montpellier provided ten thousand baths.

It is in the forties, however, when the Duchy of Lancaster took an interest, that development really starts to turn Harrogate into a major health and pleasure resort. Wells are better housed: the Improvement Commission first transfer the Sulphur Well dome and pillars to Tewit Well, then have it enclosed; St John's is improved by the same architect, Isaac Strutt, who designs the domed octagon of the Royal Pump Room in 1842. Flagged stone paving surrounds to the Pump Room are added later and the Royal Parade is also 'flagged'. The hotel and baths at Harlow Car alkaline sulphur springs are built in 1844, and the White Hart Hotel, adjacent to the Royal Parade, 'the best building in Harrogate' (Pevsner), comes in 1846. The first hotel of urban design, it has a three-storey front, arched ground-floor windows and Ionic doorway columns. The classical Crown and the Clarendon shortly follow: then, in 1855, the Queens.

It is during the forties that the houses in Westmorland Street and the Royal Parade are erected, and a building for the Magnesia Well is provided by the Commissioners. Swan Road, with late Grecian porches, has been developed a few years earlier. Crescent Road is developed in the fifties and the spa centre is then virtually complete. Victoria Avenue and the detached or semi-detached dark stone houses, in gabled Tudor or Italianate style, of the West Park area consolidate its southern flank in the next decade. The Harlow Manor Hydro, in Cold Baths Road (leading from Royal Parade), a former private house, has gables and Gothic details in true high Victorian style. Hotels proliferate: one close to the Cheltenham Spring warned its visitors that, Harrogate being a health resort, 'patrons of this hotel are not expected to use wine etc. unless they require it' and adds, 'NB No fees given to Conductor to recommend this hotel'.

Harrogate stands on a fold of Lower Carboniferous rock: it is the faulting of this rock and the exposure of the strata usually lying at a deep level that has produced the diversity and distribution of its manifold springs. Of equal, if not greater significance nowadays, for its attraction to visitors, is the fact that it stands in the old Forest of Knaresborough, of which, by provision of an Act of Parliament during the enclosures, two hundred acres were to remain forever unenclosed, primarily so that there should always be public access to the springs. This is the origin of the Stray—the town's most characteristic distinguishing feature. From 'stinted' pasture, the two hundred acres have been turned by the Corporation into large sweeps of well-kept lawn, with wedges darting right into the centre of the town. Along with the Valley Gardens (opened in 1887), the green before the Crown Hotel and that extending from the Pump Room to King's Road, Harrogate greets the eye almost everywhere with refreshing open spaces.

In defiance of certain rival Victorian resorts which deemed it suitable for invalids only from early August to mid-September, because of the risk of 'breathing its atmosphere and encountering its gales' and the possibility of rain on four days of the week, Harrogate continued to prosper famously, up to and well after the century's end. London society came for its gout, rheumatism, lumbago, liver or merely 'jangled nerves'. Faded lettering over a shop in Montpellier Parade still announces that the local paper publishes a daily list of their comings and goings. The breezy air and so-accessible grassy pleasaunces recommended it to most people; if invalids needed cosseting there was the Kursaal, built in 1905, the sumptuous sheltered grounds and interiors of international hotels like the Majestic, hugely towering in red brick, with gables and domes, just above, and the Winter Gardens, with, of course, carriages or 'Coventry chairs'—pedalled bath-chairs—from hotels to wells and baths every morning. The occasional storms were taken as a joke. 'Fearful gale yesterday. Electric lights broke down. Great fun watching the poor ladies getting blown about. They had to cling to railings etc. Saw two ladies blown head over heels. Awful joke. Alfred arrived in simply soaked, from the Majestic. George.' But the card showing the Pump Room was posted on 26 December 1902.

Harrogate 'the largest and most important spa in Great Britain: really a compendium of the world's spas—for relaxation and change, offers bracing air, beautiful country, excellent music, golf, bright society—renders the German and Austrian resorts absolutely unnecessary'. The demise of the spa life of Europe, for many British people, began when the medical profession realised how much more profitable it was to have their patients on a diet or cure at home and under their supervision, rather than to send them abroad to some watering place and split their fee with a foreign physician. When the amenities were up to continental standard, reliance could be placed on a regimen and daily round that were much the same.

At 'Arriège', for example, in 1903, 'a smell of orange-blossom and sulphur baths—the local smell. Those people, the bathers and water-drinkers, stripped us and devoured us with their cannibal eyes . . . all the tittle tattle and spying and scandalmongering going on among these people with nothing to do and riddled with boredom;' (Colette: *Claudine and Annie*). Breakfast, walk in the park, medicinal baths, douche-massage—at the hands of a sexless creature in an oil-cloth apron and wooden clogs—reading or dozing in the vestibule of the Casino, to the sound of an orchestra as drowsy as themselves: 'it is not only arthritis that ossifies so many joints here'. On the more cosmopolitan occasions at Baden-Baden, Carlsbad, Vichy, Aix-les-Bains, Wiesbaden, Bagni di Lucca (frequented by Shelley, Byron, Heine, Elizabeth Browning and burial place of 'Ouida'), Bagni di Montecatini (patronised in the 1950s by the late Duke of Windsor), Bad Homburg or Marienbad, the last two being King Edward VII's successive favourites —it was a routine of waters taken at eight, twelve and six, from different springs to which the visitor walked; afternoons of croquet, golf or driving; at meals boiled food only; music, dancing and flirtation in the Kurhaus; bed at ten. As *Punch* remarked of (Not so) Bad Homburg: 'Amount of things you are not to eat and drink amazing; some of them never tasted in my life, now strongly tempted. Hotels under sceptre of Dr Dutz. He watches over table d'hote and prevents most nice things from coming to dinner. Kurhaus always open, palatial building not to be outdone in size and beauty by Casino at Monte Carlo.'

Such spas may have served a political or social purpose for statesmen's leisurely, informal exchanges and indulged the gambler's passion, but were not different in kind from Harrogate. At the Royal Baths Neville Chamberlain took the cure—and is to be seen there in a *Punch* drawing, making a wry face. At the Kursaal distinguished pre-war (1914) audiences came for performances by Kreisler, Paderewski, Pavlova, Bernhardt and Melba. Louis Wain, the whimsical artist, obviously familiar with the Fountain Court and Lounge Hall, made a drawing of cats taking the waters at dainty little tables to the accompaniment of a feline orchestra.

Formerly the internal and external application of local waters was practically the only form of treatment in spas, apart from massage. And, apart from rheumatic disorders, the main body of complaints derived from rich living—the English habit of gluttony made possible by a combination of industrial prosperity, colonisation, imperialism and steam transport. In the early twentieth century, however, up to eighty methods of treatment were available at Harrogate, with all the advantages of a continental 'cure'. Discovery of the means of producing and applying electric currents greatly increased the range. In turn the range of diseases capable of treatment was also increased and the length of the cure shortened. Patients were attracted with a wide variety of complaints, from arthritis, gout, dyspepsia and chronic constipation to anaemia, dysentery, neurasthenia and the aftermath of tropical diseases. A Pullman service from Edinburgh to London made Harrogate its halfway stopping place and, of course, it was readily accessible to large areas of population via Leeds or en route by through train to Liverpool. About the turn of the century there was one doctor to every 300 of Harrogate's population—compared with the normal town ratio of one to 2,000—and at its peak there were one thousand treatments every day at the Royal Baths.

To some observers the essential spirit of Harrogate is late Edwardian, belonging as it does to the last leisurely age. The pattern of the streets is 'happily accidental'; in walking the town one falls 'into a meandering carefree saunter' (Pevsner). The Stray is obviously for people with time to stroll after breakfast and before dinner; the cafes for long, mid-morning chats; the shops, like seaside shops, to tempt those with time to admire curios, fashion, flower displays, antiques. Queen Mary often visited the antique shops of Montpellier Parade. In the Edwardian heyday, on fine mornings, a small orchestra played in the bandstand in Crescent Gardens, tables and chairs were placed on the pavement and road outside the Pump Room, and the whole area was closed to traffic by suspended chains—a practice which survived until World War II. The Valley Gardens and sun colonnade encourage sitting and lingering to watch the passers-by: and many of them, even today, in their date-less tweeds and deerstalkers, deep straw hats and parasols, could be mistaken for Edwardian themselves.

To some extent the spa still evokes the manners of its prime, when the main season lasted from April to November (the high season being July to October), but baths and wells and hotels were open all the year round. A Hallé concert in the Kursaal (now the Royal Hall) in a setting of gilt and red plush, caryatids and Canaletto reproductions, or tea-time in the Royal Baths Assembly Room restaurant, with its opulent fountain nymphs and flowers, its crimson columns and carpet, its steamy heat and rich cream cakes, its three-piece orchestra playing Gilbert and Sullivan and elderly, plump, white-aproned waitresses—these have the traditional atmosphere.

But Harrogate ceased to be a spa, in the true sense, in 1969, when Leeds Regional Board terminated its contract and the Royal Municipal Baths were closed for all treatment except Turkish baths. The scale of support from private patients had long since declined—latterly to 15 per cent of the total—and in therapeutic treatment for National Health patients the use of synthetic medicines gradually supplanted much of the need for spa waters, whilst baths in various forms were made available at the hospitals. The Royal Baths—once a complete balneological unit—is scheduled for redevelopment instead as a complete civic centre. Meanwhile Harrogate the resort redeploys its resources in halls and hotels for conferences, trade fairs, exhibitions and so on, and its central position and amenities for the establishment of various administrative and research headquarters. As a holiday town it mingles outdoor and indoor attractions supremely well: the spring flower season on the Stray, in the public gardens, in the trial gardens of Harlow Car and at special shows is no less magnetic to visitors than the summer festival season of music and of the arts and sciences. There are widely patronised French and Italian weeks. The Great Yorkshire Show has its permanent ground there: the quality shops in the wide streets of fine Yorkshire stone exert an all-the-year-round appeal. Like Cheltenham, Harrogate offers its shoppers free disc parking. When last the present writer was staying in Harrogate a coach from Bad Neustadt waited alongside Montpellier Gardens for its contingent from one of the hotels. Many people from abroad, as well as city-dwellers from all over the North, find in Harrogate the ideal place to breathe, shop and relax.

Ilkley, about seventeen miles from Harrogate, was fond of calling itself, in its heyday, the 'Malvern of the North': it is distinguished for its moors. Like Harrogate it began to flourish notably from the 1840s, but had neither the earlier fame nor the later standing, except in one particular respect, of that prestige resort. It was a Roman site, an important military station at the intersection of two highways, one from York to Ribchester, the other from Manchester to Aldborough. A stone figure believed to represent Verbeia, goddess of the river Wharfe, was found there, whom the people of 'Olicana' may have regarded as a goddess of healing. There was a Roman spring some way up on the moors, which by the end of the seventeenth century was used to feed a small bath built just below. The water had some repute locally— as far as Leeds and Bradford, but when it was first used for curative purposes is not known. In 1773 Ilkley is described as 'dirty and in-significant', though known to the invalid. In the 1820s it is still 'one of the most rustic, inaccessible and primitive little places in the country' and the whole of the better class of lodging houses might have been counted on one's fingers. There were no public conveyances either to or from the place.

The wells and baths were at this time rented out, there being stables beneath for visitors who wished to ride up on donkey- or pony-back and enjoy an invigorating cold immersion. The Ilkley Baths charity (in Green Lane, now The Grove) was started, to administer to sufferers aid by means of the baths and the attention of an appointed physician. In the thirties the local curate opened out the 'Canker' or Sore-eye Well, a chalybeate spring on the same lane. By this time a considerable inn had been built and also some of the houses on the road up to the Old Wells. But what really began the development of the 'Malvern of the North' took place in 1844 in the adjoining village of Wheatley. A citizen of Leeds came back from Germany with experience of the 'cold water system', with restored health and the determination that York-shire should have the benefit of the same type of treatment. He chose the Ilkley district, formed a company, appointed a Silesian physician, set him up in a boarding house and for a short time patients came there or stayed in other lodging. Then, in view of the number of patients arriving and the inadequacy of a lodging house for all the appliances needed, it was decided to build. A site was purchased at Wheatley and in May 1844 the Ben Rhydding Hydropathic Establishment opened, offering 'scientific baths of every description'. It was the pioneer of all the numerous institutions of its kind in Great Victorian Britain.

The building, to which extensions and alterations were continually made, was imposing: the promenades and views of Wharfedale from it, delightful. In the grounds 'no step can be taken without the discovery of some new beauty. We climb a steep and winding path and reach at one turn a rustic gate leading to fields intersected by walks. At another we encounter a miniature lake, with its bridge and pigmy islets: and again we come suddenly on a handsome Gothic shrine, which covers a marble lion's head, from which issues a gush of water, clear as crystal and which flows into a white marble font—the shrine and its appendages being a memorial erected by Hamer Stansfield, the founder of Ben Rhydding, in honour of Preissnitz, the great discoverer of the water

Frontispiece from *Ben Rhydding, The Asclepion of England* by Rev R. Wodrow Thomson

cure.' Before long some cleric, describing its beauties, its ways and its water cure, was calling Ben Rhydding 'The Asclepion of England' (Greek: temple of health).

For Ilkley, the effect of introducing hydropathy to the vicinity was to turn it into a popular resort. To the old village below by the parish church a spa was added, climbing up to the moor. The directory for 1838 gives only seventy names and three inns, while heather grew down to the main street and its brook: in 1900 there were at least 1,500 inhabited houses, Brook Street was one of several thoroughfares, there were numerous well-built houses, shops and hotels, avenues bordered with villas, stately residences on the hillside, huge hydros and handsome places of worship. Where there had been a small cotton mill in Wells Road there was now the Royal Hotel; Green Lane, where an old thatched cottage had been the favoured lodging of Madame Tussaud, was turned into The Grove. The architecture here is roughly contemporary with the Wells House Hydro, designed in the style of an Italian palace by Cuthbert Brodrick (architect of Leeds Town Hall) and opened in 1856. There were other hydros—Craiglands, Troutbeck, Rockwood, The Spa (temperance). The committee of the Bath charity

Troutbeck Hydropathic Establishment & Sanatorium, Ilkley, from *Shuttleworth's Guide to Ilkley*

built a hospital in The Grove in 1862 and in August 1865 the railway opened, so that the then two-hour coach journey to Leeds or Bradford was halved, an important impulse to increasing residential property. Gas lighting soon followed and houses went up in West View, Mount Pleasant and Belle Vue Terrace. Both visitors and inhabitants continued to increase by leaps and bounds, but the latter not quite so fast as the speculative building schemes. In the 1870s there was an increasing building mania, which eventually so overleaped demand that by 1880 about a hundred and fifty houses stood in want of tenants. (The inner shopping centre also seems to have been arrested in its development at some stage.) In addition to the large Congregational and Wesleyan chapels, both erected in 1869, and the later Primitive Methodist, a new church, St Margaret's, designed by Norman Shaw, was dedicated ten years later to serve the resort's needs. Its seating capacity, one thousand, was still too small for the visiting season. Nearly a dozen private schools took root and in 1893 a new grammar school was built. By the end of the century Ilkley's population was reckoned at about 7,000, a figure doubled by resident visitors in summer, to which could be added about 200,000 day-visitors each year.

For those who elected to stay 'hydropathic' in later Victorian days the outdoor diversions included tennis, rackets, croquet, fives, bowls, skittles, and, of course, walks or carriage drives to such sights as the ruins of Bolton Abbey or the 'magnificent manufactory' at Saltaire, with its princely mills and hundreds of handsome cottages for the workpeople.

Indoors there were facilities for billiards, bagatelle, chess, draughts, 'squails'—every amusement except cards. The evenings were 'rendered agreeable' by charades, games, dances (but *no* waltzing), readings, recitations and musical and other entertainments. These diversions followed tea, cocoa and toast at 7pm—a 'meal' at which evening dress was expected; at 9pm supper was served—a glass of cool, clear water. By their constant recourse to diversions the Victorians would seem to have been frightened of falling into the shallows of social intercourse rather than the depths. For those aged or lady-shunning gentlemen, however, whose modesty or misogyny rendered 'the gaieties and fascinations of the Drawing Room distasteful', a reading room was provided to complete the aims of the therapy treatment—that is to renovate the body by the application of pure water and exercise in pure air, and to relax the mind. The habit of extinguishing five out of six of the gas lights in the drawing room at 10pm as a hint to the company to disperse and then at 11pm turning the gas off and plunging public rooms, bedrooms and passages into darkness, ensured adequate rest or at any rate cessation of excitement. On Sundays, of course, the routine was adjusted so that visitors could attend morning and afternoon church services; for evening service the dining room was transformed into a

Page 85 (*above*) Malvern Priory and Abbey Hotel; (*below*) the Kursaal, Harrogate; its name was changed during World War I to Royal Hall

chapel. Testimony was quoted that of hundreds of patients 'washed and sent home' at least 90 per cent went satisfied with the system and very much improved in health.

Many of the later day-visitors came out of the cities by train and then walked over the moor—'Ilkla Moor' of the 'anthem'—to or from a hostelry known as 'Dick Hudson's'. The Local Board wisely purchased the manorial rights in 1892, along with the wooded ground of Heber's Ghyll and spring and the Panorama Rocks. So the public had access to about two thousand breezy acres. It was a saying in the district that a walk on the moors was worth a bottle of the best champagne. It also had heady possibilities for the archaeologist and historian in the discovery of ancient flints, arrowheads, carved stones, cairns and circles of Bronze Age or Celtic origin, and in contemplation of the unique Swastika Stone. The gritstone 'Cow and Calf' rocks—like the rocks at Tunbridge Wells—attracted the more venturesome. Today they and the quarry-face behind attract Sunday rock-climbers and their gallery of spectators. There is a convenient licensed house close by for those demanding champagne *and* moorland air.

The patrons of Ilkley in its heyday came from all ranks of society with the exception of royalty. The town's motto 'Per salubritatem opes' reflected the source of its prosperity. It has continued to prosper, in a different way. Whilst the hydros have either been taken down altogether and their sites, with wide views over Wharfedale, swallowed by building estates, or been converted into educational establishments or remodelled as hotels; while the railway has been closed, the 'promenades' with their seats largely neglected, the chapels either amalgamated or sorely depleted, the attraction of Ilkley has by no means diminished. As a place of residence, for a breath of moorland air, a meal out or a visit to the modern open-air lido it draws on support from a large conurbation. It is a dormitory for successful Leeds and Bradford business men, a preferred place for children's schooling, a natural anchorage for musical festivals, touring Rugby teams, tennis tournaments. Its hotels offer overnight resting-places for Highland coach tourists and old-fashioned comfort for bridge congresses and business conferences. It has just started its own Literature Festival.

Once considered 'eminently adapted for children of strumous habit,

CLOSE AND OPEN

CARRIAGES

KEPT FOR HIRE,

AT

M. HAINSWORTH'S,

WELLS TERRACE, ILKLEY.

APARTMENTS:

Splendid and uninterrupted prospect.
Close to the Moor.

Advertisement from *Shuttleworth's Guide-book to Ilkley*

and the weakly frames of children born in India of English parents', Ilkley is now regarded as a healthy and pleasant place to live for all whose lives mainly, perforce, must be spent in cities. On a hot summer's day, when the flowerbeds are in bloom, The Grove retains quite a fashionable air as a rendezvous for leisurely shoppers, public-school children and their parents, strolling enjoyers of a half-day off. For all its 'big, ugly Victorian houses' and more recent suburban spread, it has, like Ben Rhydding of old, Scottish overtones. On many a winter's day one can climb in half an hour above mist and murk level into keen air and sunshine where only grouse moors are in view.

Unlike Harrogate and Ilkley, Droitwich consists of two quite dissimilar parts. The old, formerly industrial section lies in a hollow near the river; the modern half is on high ground, with wide roads and custom-built houses in pleasant scenery. 'Salinae' to the Romans, Droitwich was dominated for centuries by the salt industry. Although the manufacture of salt has in this century been discontinued, traces of the industry may still be seen between Vines Park, alongside the river Salwarpe, and the old High Street, which itself reveals the result of years of extraction from beneath its site by the dip in the middle of its length. An old ecclesiastical-looking inn, an Elizabethan priory house of attractive black-and-white timbered design and a number of other sixteenth- and seventeenth-century houses in the Friar Street and St Andrew's Street area give this part of the town the familiar West Midlands 'magpie' look. Some buildings take up strange leaning postures owing to the former workings.

The natural springs, in which, before borings were made, the brine derived from beds of rock salt came to the surface for evaporation, gave to the old town its Anglo-Saxon name—'wich' or 'wyche', the settlement near the salt springs; the Norman 'droit' (right) indicates that they could be legally used for salt manufacture, subject to taxation. The healing virtues of the springs, discovered accidentally during a cholera epidemic in 1832, gave it both new repute and the raison d'être of new development. When cholera patients were bathed in brine, owing to a temporary shortage of fresh water, their marked improvement in health was noted; doctors repeated the treatment with other patients, with encouraging results. A company, including Lord

Hamilton, then formed to develop the remarkable properties of brine for various rheumatic ailments. In 1830 the first bathing establishment, Royal Baths, was opened. The town was well sited for invalid visitors, being sheltered by the Malvern and Lickey Hills.

Development of the modern part of the town and its facilities as a spa, however, was mainly due to the enterprise of John Corbett, who before the Queen's era, when taking the waters was still fashionable, had already realised the possibilities. Droitwich owes to Corbett, characterised as the 'salt king', some of its best hotels—including The Raven—and new roads, its fine park and Salter's Hall, in addition to the St Andrew Brine Baths, which set it up as a modest health resort. The hotels and superior boarding establishments, with their tennis and croquet lawns, heated corridors and bedrooms 'on the ground floor if desired', the golf course and the daily orchestra in the park, conformed to pattern. Corbett's own mansion, at Dodderhill, built of red brick and Bath stone, in the style of a French chateau for his French wife, has also been turned into a hotel. At the end of the Victorian era the baths again had to be extensively improved: St John's Brine Baths Hospital, partly supported by voluntary contributions, served the needs of poorer patients.

The 'Brine Spa' finally took over from the 'salt town' in 1922, by which time the works had been dismantled, the town replanned and the industry removed altogether to Stoke Prior. The brine is unique—though Nantwich, another old salt town, also has brine baths—with a concentration ten times that of sea-water and a buoyancy which enables one to float like a cork, lie back to rest or walk around the heated swimming bath without touching bottom. If you are a cyclist and want a simple method of progression you perform a pedalling motion with your feet and away you go. It is infectious as well as exhilarating, an entertainment as well as a cure. Athletes in training patronised Droitwich to tone up their muscular systems, as well as those seeking treatment for gout, sciatica, lumbago, arthritis and fibrositis or muscular re-education after injury to limbs. The brine was used only externally, in pool, bath, douche or pack. One employs here the past tense, since by the time this account appears in print Birmingham Regional Hospital Board may have installed hospital facilities for National

Health patients (as happened at Harrogate), in which event the Brine Baths will have to close.

Droitwich has other resort attractions of a conventional kind—ample accommodation in first-class hotels, gardens and a wooded park in the town centre, an open-air swimming lido which reproduces the salinity of the Mediterranean, a theatre and arts club. There are also fishing, hunting and racing opportunities nearby. As the hotel centre of the Midlands, it is a natural rendezvous for conferences, bridge congresses and other social functions. The climate is mild—yuccas and bamboo flourish in the gardens—and the townscape, viewed from the bluff of Dodderhill, has an agreeably rural character. Whether the character of the borough can be preserved when the planned expansion to a town of 30,000, with the provision of 6,000 additional dwellings and commerce and industry to match, takes place in the next decade, remains in question. Its planners express hope.

'The beauties of Matlock far exceeded my expectation . . . a narrow place between two rocks leads into another and larger amphitheatre, but covered with woods: in the bottom runs the river, trees and shrubs to the water's edge. At the end of this delightful place stands Matlock—a village on the banks of the Daren, consisting of neat detached houses for the company in the season, most of them white which makes a pretty contrast to the neighbouring woods . . . very pleasant "Adam's Walks" cut through the woods and leading to views of little cascades and other romantic scenes—and to the Slag mines. The lead ore of this mine seems very rich.'

Matlock was a place to visit two hundred years ago, as Silas Neville shows, if only to see Richard Arkwright's cotton mill, built in 1771, at nearby Cromford—the largest mill in England and the first mechanised textile factory in the world. It had then its two or three baths of thermal water, rising from springs under strong arches, a long room for dinners in the season and a well of pure, limpid drinking water. The special qualities of the tepid springs, issuing from limestone in the gorge south of High Tor, seem to have been noticed first by miners in about 1690. In the caverns, Rutland and Masson, near the Heights of Abraham, the Romans had once had lead workings.

The initiative of Sir Richard Arkwright in promoting the construction of a road between Belper and Cromford, later extending to Matlock Bridge and becoming a public highway in 1818, did much to overcome Matlock's earlier inaccessibility. More visitors were encouraged to come for the medicinal waters (temperature a constant 68° F) and to see the petrifying wells and the 'tufa' rock, formed by the water's action on moss and other plants. They craned their necks in wonder at the High Tor, that commanding limestone mass towering over the dale between Matlock Bath and Matlock Town, or peered from its summit into the gorge below Masson Hill (1,100 feet). Its attractions began to compete with those of Buxton and Leamington. When the Midland railway came, in 1849, from Derby along the Derwent Valley to Rowsley, still more visitors sought the growing resort. From the town, however, they did *not* see Riber Castle, with its gaunt and embattled facade looking down from a height of 800 feet facing Masson Hill. The reason was not that it had been demolished, but that it was yet to be built.

The builder was John Smedley (1803–74), a local textile manufacturer, whose company still operates in the district, but whose signal distinction was his propagandist enthusiasm for hydropathy. This was to lead to the real fame of Matlock, after the establishment at Matlock Bank of Smedley's Hydro in 1852. (The soft water supplies for this—and other hydros that followed—were drawn, not from the limestone, but from the junction of gritstone and shales on the moor above the town.) Riber Castle, in which Mr Smedley lived in the 'not inconsiderable splendour' afforded by his success in hosiery and hydropathy, was erected for him ten years later.

The fashionable era of Smedley's Hydro—an imposing building of vast proportions halfway up the bank—already seems almost as remote as that of Arkwright and his Willersley Castle on Cat Tor. Up to the period of World War I the hydro had a staff of over fifty trained male and female nurses, masseurs and bath attendants, regular consulting and resident physicians, and a daily average of two hundred and forty visitors for its unrivalled suite of hydropathic baths, electric appliances and two hundred and sixty bedrooms. It was patronised all the year round by both patients and pleasure-seekers, who could be whisked away from its genteel relaxations to the golf links 'by motor service'. 'Great Britain's Greatest Hydro' then lived up to its name: it even had a twin—The Smedley Hydropathic at Southport, for either summer holiday or winter residence, which advertised 'hydropathy fully treated' as though it were a complaint. Among other hotels and hydros that had been spawned in Matlock itself, Lilybank, Rockside, Chesterfield House, Matlock House, Oldham House, offered terms on a suitably descending scale.

Matlock House opened in 1857 and, for those wishing to enjoy the 'bracing, salubrious, recuperative and tonic air' of its elevated position, later advertised ('a cable car passes the door every few minutes') the tram service from Matlock Bridge to Matlock Bank. A coloured card, postmarked 1912, with the message to 'Dear Edith'—'Arrived safely, enjoying myself fine! How do you like this place?'—shows the extensive grounds of Chesterfield House, flags flying, fountains playing, lawn tennis courts and long verandah overlooking it, with strollers and croquet players and vintage motor-cars everywhere in cheerful evidence. The 'Drawing Room' at Oldham House, where another of Edith's correspondents, Bella, seems to have stayed, is shown on another pre-war card. Red-plush sofa and 'sociable', bamboo reclining chairs and balloon-back occasional chairs, upright piano and potted palms, several writing tables, family portraits on the walls, fitted carpets and windows with stained glass, ensured her home-from-home comfort. Terms here, until mid-wartime, were five or six shillings per day, inclusive; at Smedley's, from 8s 6d to 12s, with no extra charge for baths, Turkish or hydropathic.

Matlock is no longer in the hydropathic business: its motto 'Aquae salubritas usu' is irrelevant. The 'Fountain Baths'—one of several in Matlock Bath, formerly used for taking or bathing in the 'waters'— have become an aquarium; the caves, fissures, underground streams and petrifying wells have been commercialised to form the basis of popular entertainment. At Matlock Bank Smedley's Hydro now houses Derbyshire County Council offices, Rockside is occupied by a College of Education and Riber Castle, after a period as a school, has been turned into a zoo. Willersley Castle is a Wesley Guild holiday centre. Textile and engineering activities have expanded and quarrying work has extended its disfiguring scars. But in spite of this, the natural attractions noted by Neville largely remain and, coupled with artificial 'improvements', keep many smaller hotels and guest houses in business for the resort, as well as for Matlock the excursion centre.

The Matlocks, 'the area of a thousand views', still have a setting of green trees and hills, of grey and white cliffs and crags 'the tossed and stony ocean nearing The moment to o'erwhelm us all' (John Betjeman). Their situation, in fact, is more striking than the townships themselves. There are the wooded Heights of Abraham, given their name by an officer who fought with Wolfe at Quebec, and Victoria Prospect Tower, commanding a splendid panorama from the hill crest. High Tor, 350 feet above the Derwent and Matlock Dale, remains picturesque despite the railway (now closed) popping in and out of tunnels along its length; the leafy winding Via Gellia (not a Roman road, but named after its makers the Gell family) opens beyond Cromford; the Black Rocks with their gullies and gritstone buttresses attract climbers. These scenes charm by their variety in summer and, under a winter blanket of snow, give to the district aspects of a miniature Switzerland. A network of paths enables the visitor to explore the whole area in comfort.

The intersecting Lovers' Walks, and Hall Leys public gardens, the outdoor swimming pool and the indoor occasions of the Grand Pavilion (and former Pump Room), these are among the 'improvements' and are all within easy reach for those who have strolled along South Parade and the Promenade at Matlock Bath, seen the thermal water fountain and fishpond, admired Artists' Corner, the 'Romantic Rocks' and Speedwell Cavern. A Venetian fete, with illuminations, decorated boats on the Derwent and fireworks, also brings in a big concourse of visitors from late August until October. More so than Buxton, Matlock has become a 'popular' resort and caters for popular tastes: its added amenities and recent growth reflect the measure of its success.

Matlock hotels, of course, can still offer the unique provision of warm indoor and outdoor swimming pools fed by thermal springs. But today the former spa's chief association with the virtues and rites of water is of far more antique origin than hydropathy. The ceremony of well-dressing, with the processions and triptych flower panels at well-heads, probably has medieval ancestry, even links with similar rites practised by the ancient Greeks. Local communities have benefited from time immemorial from the unfailing supply of water from the deeper wells and a number of the villages surrounding Matlock, or within easy range in the Peak National Park, recognise this by keeping up the rites annually on various special days. Visitors can take their choice from at least a dozen places—Ashford-in-the-Water, Barlow, Bonsall, Bradwell, Dore, Endon, Eyam, Hope, Litton, Stoney Middleton, Tideswell, Tissington, Wirksworth, Wormhill, Youlgrave.

At Tissington (referred to on p. 49) the ceremony appears to have been revived in 1615, when in the great drought lasting from 25 March to 4 August its five wells continued to flow when all other wells had run dry. In gratitude the villagers decorated them with all the best that could be culled from garden, field and hedgerow and the practice became an annual Ascension Day festival. Other well-dressings are revivals, some entirely modern—not on the limestone and not free from a suggestion of commercialism. As a postscript to Matlock Spa, however, the tradition—with the procession, church service, blessing of the well and biblical tapestry picture and text, made up from flower petals, leaves and seeds pressed into a bed of clay then mounted on a wooden frame—vividly serves to recall the unchanging mystery of waters under the earth.

Chapter Six

SPA-LETS

THE FOLLOWING inquiry, made of the clergy for each parish in northern Britain, in 1771, was appended to Pennant's *Tour in Scotland*:

> Are there any mineral springs, frequented for the drinking of the waters; what are they; at what season of the year are they reckoned best, and what distempers are they frequented for?
>
> Are there any hot waters or wells for bathing and for what distempers frequented?
>
> Are there any petrifying springs or waters that incrust bodies; what are they?

The age, to say the least, had water on the mind. Whatever the inquiry disclosed it is evident that during the course of the late eighteenth and early nineteenth centuries nearly every suitable township, or even village of enterprise and ingenuity, managed to find what it was looking for in the way of beneficial, and profitable, wells or springs. Not all were inland, not all developed into resorts—or, if they did, lasted longer than the first fashionable phase—not all survived rivalry by larger or luckier neighbours, and not all have left much of interest, even in the way of tradition, for present-day inquirers. 'I am persuaded that there are fifty spaws in England as efficacious and salutary as Scarborough, though they have not yet risen to fame: and perhaps never will, unless some medical encomist should find an interest in displaying their virtues to the public view. Be that as it may, recourse will always be had to *this* place for the convenience of sea-bathing, while this practice prevails' (Tobias Smollett, 1771). The vagaries of fashion, in medicine as in anything else, being what they are, it was as well for a place to get on the water 'wagon' whilst that particular practice did prevail and the public was ready to swallow.

Double Smollett's 'fifty', and one has a conservative estimate of the number of British towns which once claimed to be fully fledged 'spaws', quite a number of which lasted out the nineteenth century. When the North Eastern Railway, for example, advertised around 1890 tourist tickets to *Ilkley, Ben Rhydding, Harrogate, Scarborough*, Whitby, Robin Hood's Bay, Filey, Bridlington, Hornsea, Withernsea, Seaton Carew, *Redcar*, Saltburn-by-the-Sea, Hartlepool (East), Sunderland, *Croft*, Richmond, Appleby, Barnard Castle, South Shields, Tynemouth, Cullercoats, Whitley, *Hexham, Gilsland*, Alston, Newbiggin-by-the-Sea, Bilton (for Alnmouth), Wooler and Berwick, eight of these places (italicised) were resorts recognised for their waters. To them might have been added Knaresborough. Towards the end of World War I the West and South Clare Railways put out an advertisement headed 'STRAFE GERMANY'—'by visiting Kilkee, Spanish Point, Lahinch and Lisdoonvarna'. The latter then claimed that its sulphur and iron spa was equal, and in some respects superior, to Harrogate, while Kilkee at least had now 'an abundant supply of good pure water and new sanitation arrangements'. These were among the more widely known resorts: at one time Greater London had over half a dozen separate resorts within its boundaries. To them could be added scores with only local repute or of the kind that remained 'undeveloped'—Ashton, Bolemore, Codsalwood, Haigh, Kedleston, Kilburn, Kirby, Luz, their name is legion. When resorts sought to provide in their most highly finished shape 'the amusements of which high society is especially fond', this required recognition of the commercial possibilities, speculation and building enterprise, medical support, astute public relations—perhaps the 'draw' of a popular preacher or of a public school—or proximity to a large town, to establish the place on a profitable and permanent footing. The early bloom of the 'also-rans' perforce faded without leaving much trace, at any rate of the kind that is sought by the industrial archaeologist.

It would be impracticable here to detail the whole diaspora of 'spa-lets' over two or more centuries or the places which boasted a 'spa' in the sense of a mineral water spring. A sample of the older and of the later, of the metropolitan and of the humbly local will serve to indicate their range and interest.

'There is a little steele water much frequented by the gentry, it has some mixture of allum not so strong as Tunbridge and there is a fine Gravell Walke that is between high cutt hedges where is a Roome for the Musick and a Roome for the Company beside the Private Walkes: the well issues not very quick . . . full of moss's which is all changed yellow by the water' (Celia Fiennes). The well, St Rumbold's at Astrop (the 'baby' saint had others at Brackley and Buckingham) had had a healing tradition for the lame and blind since the middle ages: their 'superstitious practice' had been censured and prohibited by the bishop of the diocese in 1280; the medicinal properties had been 'dis-covered' by a 'learned physician' in 1668; and, supported by the testi-mony of a certain Dr Radcliffe of Oxford, only some fourteen miles away, Astrop's well again became a place of pilgrimage. Up to the mid-eighteenth century there was a ball every Monday, and public breakfast, cards and dancing every Friday during the season; visitors included Anthony Wood and Lord and Lady Gainsborough; it was one of the most fashionable places of resort in England . . . The tide turned: Dr Radcliffe withdrew his support, and by 1777 Astrop had lost its repute. A small well of chalybeate water, roughly edged with stone, and a rustic bench were all that served a century later to remind people of St Rumbold and his water's healing powers.

Alford in 'Summersetshire', about two miles from Castle Cary, was another seventeenth-century possessor of 'a mineral water which Com-pany resorts to for drinking'; by Celia Fiennes's time it had lost some of its earlier popularity. There was insufficient accommodation for people of Fashion: instead one sent for the water to brew beer. The city of Wells, of course, derives its name from the springs near the cathedral: a water conduit from St Andrew's Well feeding the streets made the medieval city unusually hygienic—though it did not turn it into a watering place. Melksham, however, in the neighbouring county, did try to set up as a spa and Holt, a few miles off, succeeded for a time. Both have attractive period houses: a fine crescent and converted pump room remain as characteristic witnesses to Melksham's ambition.

Bristol Hotwell was extensively patronised at about the same period as Astrop. The diarist Evelyn recorded the water's special clearness, warmth and sweetness. The well was at the foot of the precipitous St Vincent Rocks, beneath the present suspension bridge, where people went searching for diamonds. A spa was formed and from about 1690 to 1790 remained fashionable and crowded, figuring along with Bath in the novels of Smollett and Jane Austen. Silas Neville drank his glass of water at the Pump Room and saw 'everything remarkable' in Bristol. Smollett enjoyed the fine air on Clifton Downs, found that the ships and boats going up and down the river, close under the windows of the Pump Room, afforded 'an enchanting variety of *moving pictures*', but always returned low-spirited. He was put off by the poor emaciated creatures there in the last stages of consumption 'like so many exotic plants languishing in a hothouse' and by the stink, caused by the mud and slime left at low ebb and so prejudicial to the 'ghostly company's' weak lungs. Of the waters, his opinion as a doctor—he had also stayed at Lucca, Italy—was that they could have but little effect on the 'animal oeconomy'—containing nothing but salt and calcarious earth, though perhaps they might be of some service for diabetes, diarrhoea and night sweats. Soon after the beginning of the nineteenth century fashion deserted Bristol and visitors started to settle around the little village of Clifton, above the gorge, where many literary celebrities made their home. By 1860 it had become a town of 15,000 'built with every reference to its health capabilities'. Fashion has stayed with Clifton amidst its elegant terraces, Crescent and Paragon.

The 'spaw well' at Scarborough was on the sand by the sea-shore, 'something from an iron or steele mineral'. The first spa buildings were erected about 1700, half a century before the new sea-bathing era: the curvaceous outline of the Crescent, including Wood End, once residence of the Sitwell family, now a museum, suggests a Bath importation; below is the Rotunda. The best lodgings, according to Celia Fiennes, were in Quakers' hands. As happened elsewhere, Scarborough's waters were denounced as spurious by a physician who championed those of Knaresborough, but in any case Smollett had detected a falling off in Scarborough's reputation by the 1770s.

Canterbury was at first almost as well patronised as Tunbridge for its chalybeate spring; it had fine walks, seats and places for music and was 'comodious to the Company'. Barnet and Epsom also had plenty of early patrons. Their waters were similar. Barnet had a very sharp air and was a large place with plenty of accommodation. Pepys took his three glasses there, but in general it was frequented by the poorer classes, as was Dulwich or Woodford Wells, while the wealthy were patronising Tunbridge and the middle classes Epsom. Epsom, like Barnet, was not a quick spring and was very often drunk dry, the usual way of drinking being to 'turn' the water with a little milk. Assembly Rooms were built in 1706 and a new well sunk, but it had to be supplemented with water brought from the common wells to fill it in the mornings, and, being therefore weak and inefficacious, it discredited the older one. There were many brick houses with gardens and courtyards available for lodging, a coffee house, gaming rooms, fruit and sweetmeat shops and two greens. The Upper Green was for bowling and promenading, the Lower, in the heart of the town, offered gaming houses, milliners' and china shops, and a piazza. Pepys in his time enjoyed much mirth in the Courtyard and Bowling Green at Durdans (belonging to Lord Barkeley), but found later that 'citizens', not 'quality', composed the greatest part of the company—he wondered where they got the means and the notion to go there and what they did with their time.

Thomas Shadwell, the subject of one of Dryden's satires, produced a play, *Epsom Wells*; and, if further éclat were needed, racing on the downs had been the fashion there since the time of James I. The first Derby was run in 1780.

Hampstead, long before it became 'appy, had an era of spa-dom. Well Walk, off East Heath Road in Old Hampstead, passes the site of the wells that made it a fashionable eighteenth-century resort. Silas Neville was one of those who sought out Hampstead and also Kilburn Wells, walking over the fields in summer and then returning by the turnpike through Paddington. He found the excursion very pleasant and free of dust, but Hampstead was 'too near the capital and full of its follies and ridiculous characters'. The site of Wells Hotel adjoins that of the house where Keats lodged; Flask Walk is another reminder of the 'cure' days. It is, however, as the finest 'lung' in the London neighbourhood, by its summer fair near the Vale of Health, and with its artistic associations, that Hampstead keeps its resort tradition alive.

Closer in to the City, Beaulah Spa (Sydenham), Sadlers Wells, Islington Spa, Clerkenwell, Shadwell and St Bride's were among the places of resort for the citizens of former centuries. Beaulah Spa, first discovered in 1678, was subsequently revived and became fashionable, with entertainments and dancing. Its waters, hawked through the London streets as a 'cure-all', were supplied also to St Bartholomew's Hospital. Similarly the waters of St Bride's Well, a 'sainted fluid', were bottled and, at the coronation of King George IV, purveyed by a certain Mr Walker of Blackfriars. At Clerkenwell, where the healing waters were on tap, the Pump had to be re-sited in 1800 'for the better accommodation of the neighbourhood'. Sadler's Wells, discovered in 1683, was a popular spa before it became a famous theatre. Its ferruginous waters, in the gardens of Mr Thomas Sadler, were sought by as many as six hundred visitors daily for a 'cure' claimed to be efficacious for the early stages of consumption, scurvy, diabetes, gravel, stone, and all 'hectic and hypochondriacal heat'. The company, no doubt, drank much more than water in the pleasure grounds and, as the élite of Georgian society flocked there, the rival resorts, Epsom and Tunbridge, denounced the Islington Spa as a 'plot' (fake). The district still retains some terraces of eighteenth- and early nineteenth-century houses and, after its period of decline like other purlieus on the rim of London's saucer, such as Camden Town, has now returned to fashion as a residential area. Mr Sadler's 'Musick Theatre' near the site of the medicinal springs was rebuilt in 1931. The headquarters of the Metropolitan Water Board, fittingly, are situated close by.

Claims of all kinds were made for local waters in the heyday of 'cure' belief. Some still feature among the 'sights' for visitors, like Hopton springs, mineral and formerly curative, at Ashwell, near Baldock. Gerrards Cross earned as a guide-book sobriquet 'The Brighton of Bucks', jointly for its healthy altitude (300 feet) and the water from the village pump, people coming from far and near to drink it for rheumatism. Gayhurst, a tiny village of four farms, sixteen cottages, one public house and the great house, had a chalybeate spring and was an eighteenth-century spa in a small way with its Bath House and regular patronage. Dorton chalybeate, in the same county, earned a booklet on its medicinal properties and had both a Pump Room and bathing rooms and 'other conveniences'. The well was in the corner of a pasture adjoining the grounds of Dorton House, in a secluded situation near Brill, some fifty miles from London. Its waters had a peculiar odour and a strong inky taste—indeed, with an infusion of gall, it became a good ink. It was used, however, not only as a cure for cattle mange, but for human sufferers from eye inflammation, St Vitus's dance, palsy, palpitation, flatulence, sterility and convalescence—especially on a return from the Tropics. Not a few celebrated cures were attributed to Dorton water—including a case of bleeding cancer —and in the early nineteenth century there were plans to develop twelve acres about the Pump Room for pleasure grounds. Nowadays its surest claim to attention would be proximity to Brill, one of the county's loveliest villages, once the site of a royal palace—Henry II kept court there—and with views of the most picturesque description over nine counties. The restored seventeenth-century post mill on the hill is its landmark.

Of later development than any of the foregoing, Tenbury Wells, in the Midlands, still preserves the atmosphere of a minor spa town. Its saline springs were discovered in 1839, a Pump Room was erected and as the London to North Wales coaches had a stopping place there some popularity accrued to it. The black-and-white Royal Oak and the timber-framed King's Head remind one of the coaching days. When Tuesday's produce market is held, in a round brick hall opposite the Cage Hotel, there are also Women's Institute stalls in the old pump room. Its Victorian-Gothic gables, spires and ogee windows in rusting sheet-metal face across a trout stream. A broad, slow-paced high street, a scattering of antique shops, a medieval three-arched bridge over the Teme and a position between the orchards of Herefordshire and the hopfields of Worcestershire add to the attractiveness of this spa-let.

Over the county border and a few miles into Shropshire there is

Page 103 (above) Spa Well, Low Harrogate in 1829, from a lithograph by J. Stubbs; (below) 'The Chalybeate Well at Harrogate'—the John Well—in 1796; the present building was erected in 1842. From a mezzotint by John Raphael Smith

Page 104 (above) An engraving of Dinsdale Spa, Durham; (below) an engraving of Gilsland Spa, Cumberland

another resort for the Midlander, Church Stretton—the 'Shepwardine' of Mary Webb's novels. Although it has a Norman church and one or two eighteenth-century oak-panelled houses in the tiny market square, Church Stretton's development was late nineteenth century, when it became quite a fashionable place. Sandford Avenue, the chief shopping street, and much of the half-timbered architecture is of that period. There are spring waters of a purity to rival Malvern's, a public fountain and a bottling factory, but the main attractions are outside the rather soporific little town. The walking country of the Long Mynd and Caer Caradoc, the valleys—Cardingmill, Ashes Hollow and Callow Hollow—with their clear streams and small waterfalls, the views westward to Wales and eastward to the Malverns, attract visitors both in and out of season. For the golfer there is the well-known 'mountain' course, claiming to be one of England's most elevated (1,200ft). Church Stretton still affects the manners of a resort with an annual Arts and Music Festival, a 'nature trail' in Rectory Wood, a traction-engine gymkhana, a 'season' for the many boarding houses in the town itself and in the neighbouring villages, Little and All Stretton. Its mild climate provides an incentive to longevity for its many retired settlers.

Ashby-de-la-Zouch, whose waters pumped up from deep coal pits at Moira were discovered about 1820, failed to fulfil the hopes of its becoming a fashionable resort, although well-appointed baths, a large hotel and comfortable residences for visitors were built with 'grounds for exercising well laid out'. Even in 1860 it could not be called a well-frequented place.

One of the latest, if not *the* latest, resort of this type to be developed was Woodhall Spa, Lincolnshire. The mineral springs were discovered in 1811 during boring operations for coal and there is some Georgian building at the rear of the spa premises; although of limited fame by 1860, the resort developed from the 1890s and is mainly early twentieth century in architecture. A pump room was built in the surrounding pinewoods, five large hotels sprang up (one being abandoned by its German owner in 1914, another, the Victoria, being burnt down in 1918) and a long tree-lined street of shops was laid out, with a church at either end. The one in use, St Peter's (1893), brick both inside and out, is by Hodgson Fowler and faces the black-and-white half-timbered

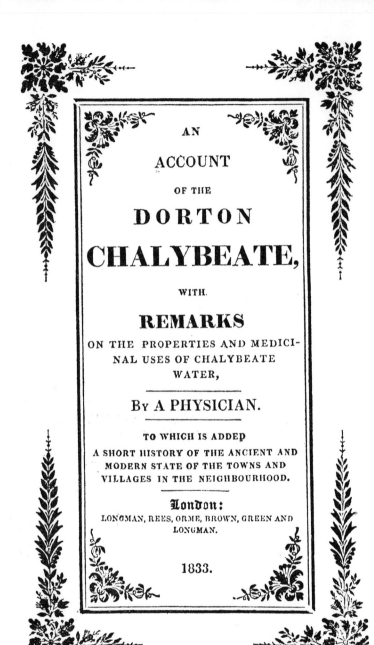

AN

ACCOUNT

OF THE

DORTON

CHALYBEATE,

WITH

REMARKS

ON THE PROPERTIES AND MEDICI-
NAL USES OF CHALYBEATE
WATER,

By A PHYSICIAN.

TO WHICH IS ADDED

A SHORT HISTORY OF THE ANCIENT AND
MODERN STATE OF THE TOWNS AND
VILLAGES IN THE NEIGHBOURHOOD.

London:

LONGMAN, REES, ORME, BROWN, GREEN AND
LONGMAN.

1833.

H. BRADFORD, PRINTER, THAME.

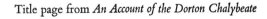

Title page from *An Account of the Dorton Chalybeate*

Golf Hotel by R. A. Cann. The large, low, timbered Petwood House was lent to replace the Victoria hotel and continues so, crowded with luxurious Edwardian furniture. With its golf course, unique Kinema-in-the-Woods, its Jubilee Park (1935) and its many large houses standing in their own wooded grounds, Woodhall Spa might be a less plushy part of Surrey, situated as it is on 'blown sand' and surrounded by heather, conifers, silver birches and rhododendrons. The black-and-white timbered effects look their age and period, especially in contrast with the finer ones of Tenbury Wells; development remains sparse.

The waters, discovered when it was hoped to find coal, contain 'free iodine' and bromine and are peculiar to Woodhall, though similar to those of Kreuznach. They have been found beneficial for sufferers from gout, rheumatism and chronic arthritis: the County Health Service still makes good use of the baths in co-operation with Sheffield Regional Hospital Board. Woodhall Spa, though sharing in Lincolnshire 'goneness', is in fact a going concern and as, climatically, it ranks as one of the four healthiest places in Britain, it attracts the well-to-do retired who look for a certain degree of restful, rural simplicity. For those who come on holiday, in addition to golf, swimming, fishing, cricket and caravan club rallies, there are wood-land and bird-watching attractions. Wax-wings, green woodpeckers, nightingales and brown squirrels are resident or regular visitors. The whole area, of course, with its variations from dry blown sand to chalk, clay and bog, is most rewarding to the botanist.

The north of England has had many spa-lets, in likely and some unlikely places, even thicker on the ground, if anything, than in the Midlands. Several were developed into attractive resorts and have interesting survivals or associations. Others remained undeveloped or unknown and frequented only by local people, until well within memory.

Boston Spa, near Tadcaster, had its origin in 1744, being known then and well on into the following century, as Thorp Spa. There is a Georgian inn, the Royal, a number of handsome, stone-built Georgian houses with bow or bay windows and columned porches along the High Street and an air of spaciousness, dignity and cleanliness to recall the days when gentry came to take the waters. Croft Spa, a village bestriding the Tees, near Darlington, was another eighteenth-century northern resort, whose rambling Spa Hotel with its three bay pediment (fronting on the A167) and the sprinkling of Queen Anne and Georgian houses suggest the days of its greater importance, when bottled aperient spa waters from its two wells were sent up to London. Associations with 'Lewis Carroll', creator of *Alice in Wonderland*, lend Croft additional interest. The celebrated writer was twelve years old when his father, the Reverend Charles Dodgson, settled into the rectory, which he occupied from 1843 to 1868. Harrogate's rise, however, and mid-Victorian predominance was Croft's downfall. The same might be said, in less positive terms, of the cathedral city of Ripon at a later date. The Spa Hotel here in Park Street was opened in 1909 for those who came to take the waters. The Spa Baths and Spa Gardens and Pump Room keep alive the tradition, but Ripon, with Harrogate so near, never really succeeded in becoming a watering place. Copgrove Spa, about six miles north-east of Harrogate—known to Celia Fiennes as Cockgrave 'where is a spring of exceedingly cold water (it shuts up the pores of the body immediately) called St Manger's [Mungo's] Well, which the Papists made use of very much'—and Knaresborough's sulphur spring, Pump Room and Baths—at Starbeck—have also faded, partly by reason of their proximity to the major spa. For its other considerable attractions, however, including the Dripping Well, Knaresborough, 'the most picturesque town in the county', remains a popular seasonal resort.

A little to the south of Teesside airport, Low Dinsdale had mineral wells which once promised to make it a little Harrogate. An engraved view by Thomas Allom (1833) shows Regency company strolling along a grassy terrace beside the ornamental water, gossiping on the benches or pointing out to each other the wooded beauties of the spa scene. There is a manor house and a twelfth-century church (restored in 1875), and, in 1860, there was a 'magnificent' hotel, but those who now seek out Dinsdale for their health's sake usually do so in order to play golf. At Gilsland in Cumberland, a small village on the river Irthing and close to a section of Hadrian's Wall, Sir Walter Scott met his bride, Charlotte Carpenter, and later paid a visit to the well and spa, fairly well developed for relaxation and social intercourse by

1830. Another of Allom's engravings shows people taking the waters at Gilsland and promenading along the waterside to a small pavilion. The custom here too merited a Spa Hotel which overlooks a deep gorge, and, as I found, still has a well-booked season. On the wall of a house at Gilsland Bridge one may descry, in faded letters, the words BATH HOUSE. Haydon Bridge and Hexham, in the same area, have resort traditions, the latter possessing a hydro-'Tyndale Hydropathic Mansion'—and adding steeplechase meetings to the allure of its 'unsurpassed purity of air' and beautiful setting. The sign HAYDON SPA occurs by the riverside, a few miles west of Hexham on the A69.

'To one who has never been in this district before first impressions may not prove favourable. The appearance of the country after leaving Shap station is rather bare and it becomes more so before the hotel is reached.' As one of the wildest-looking of English main roads traverses Shap summit, this is not an overstatement (Pennant found it more black, dreary and melancholy than any of the Highland hills): but once past the Granite Polishing Works and off the north-bound highway, 'the Shap Hotel (built by the Earl of Lonsdale) bursts into view, snugly nestling amid its woods and flower gardens, encircled by an amphitheatre of hills—a veritable oasis amid the surrounding waste of moorland'. The spa flourished modestly from about 1840 and in the 1890s was attracting up to seventy guests at the height of the season.

For what did they all come to this 'secluded spot amid the heathery wild'? Primarily to 'rest and be thankful' away from the City's smoke and din, and for the mild saline waters—though the odour, 'reminding one of the smell of a gun-barrel immediately after it has been discharged', could hardly be counted in their favour. Dr Alderson, an eminent physician of the day, found the spring most genial and sanative 'for that peculiar class of diseases which intemperance and luxury engender', disorders of the liver, dyspepsia and the like. George Moore, a London merchant, testified that when harassed by his violent headaches a visit to Shap 'always did him a world of good'. In short, it offered the ideal pick-me-up for the tired business man and diner-out. For distraction and amusement, apart from the heather and rocks and the wind over the mountains, there were the usual croquet lawn, bowling green and tennis court, excellent trout fishing and no 'no trespass' notices to inhibit rambling—to Wasdale Crag, Black Dub or Docker Force. An octagonal pillar, commemorating Queen Victoria's accession, with bas reliefs of the goddess Hygeia and of the British Lion

The Pump, Shap Spa, Westmorland, from *Handy Guide to the English Lakes*

(gratuitously contributed by a self-taught artist) and the ruined tower of Shap Abbey were the landmarks. For the rest, when sated with the Pump and relaxed by the Bath 'the company generally resolve themselves into a Mutual Amusement Association, with song, readings, an occasional dance and the music of two pianos "the world forgetting by the world forgot" '.

The Furness area had its shrines of Hygeia too—at Holywell Spa, near Cartmel and at Conishead Priory. Holywell, traditionally of St Agnes, supplied water similar to that of Wiesbaden, for rheumatic Cumberland miners and casual visitors to the cottage by the spring under Humphrey Head. This continued up to World War I, but no enterprising spirit came to exploit the surroundings and turn the district, 'Rougholme', into a resort. Conishead mansion, to the south of Ulverston, was erected as a private residence in 1821, at a cost of £140,000, its 'Gothic fantasies congealed into stone' being on the ruins of a priory of Black Canons. In 1878 it was acquired by a development company, fitted with suites of baths and opened as a splendid hydro. Its extensive grounds, gardens and shrubberies, its parkland in which trees planted by the monks still flourished and its climate, 'one of the best in England', recommended it to those who fancied enjoying the right to reside in such a mansion on any terms whatever. So powerful a preacher, one might say, had been John Smedley 'the high priest of hydropathy', that converts were still ready to flock in. This 'paradise of Furness' later became a Durham miners' convalescent home: as a building it remains essentially a relic of the 'picturesque mood'.

Spa-lets were such a mixture of the pretentious and the pseudo in their latter-day of fashion that it is not an easy matter to exclude any number of quite minor places, some mere adopters of the popular label. Halifax folk, for instance, would resort to Horley Green Spaw, which merited a booklet *c* 1840: Leeds citizens might seek Calverley, Doncaster or Wakefield people Askern: Bradfordians—perhaps on their way to 'Dick Hudson's' and Ilkley Moor—might call at Bingley iron 'spaw'. Lancashire also had its local resorts—one earned a skit on 'Boilton Spaw' in the *Lonsdale Magazine*. Perhaps the valediction of a local historian to Luddenden Dean Spa which had its eccentric 'character' and holiday crowds, is most generally appropriate: 'Like many things of olden time the Spa has lost its attractiveness, but the presence of the spring, in the middle of the stream, as it were, yet untouched by it in dry weather, may still be seen: its waters have scarcely a palatable flavour.'

Chapter Seven

WELLS IN WALES

'WHY SHOULD holiday-seekers ever risk the intolerable heat of Spa or Ems, the fashion of Homburg, or the gaiety of Baden when in a few hours they can drink waters till they are tired of them on the hills of lovely Wales?' (Clement Scott). Why, indeed, unless they are not among those who want rest and simplicity of surroundings and comparative rustification, but actually prefer a taste of gay life, fashionable crowds, even an un-British degree of heat when on holiday. Yet no doubt it was the contrast to the 'blare and dreary round of so-called amusements' in the bigger places that first recommended the quiet countryside and natural pleasures of the principal Welsh spas—to others, that is, besides the natives of the Principality. The contrast was also accompanied by a welcome economy and avoidance of tedious travel.

Situated within a few miles of each other and accessible, in their prime, by the LNWR which passed through the heart of the wells district and might be said to 'tap' all the spas in succession, the Welsh resorts taken from north to south comprised Llandrindod Wells, Builth, Llangammarch Wells and Llanwrtyd Wells. Builth is on the Wye, Llandrindod on its tributary the Ithon, the remaining two on another tributary, the Irfon. Of their bracing situation, clean air and lovely surroundings in Breconshire and Radnorshire, still two of the most sparsely populated counties (Radnor: 37 to 1 square mile) there could be no dispute. The oldest, Llanwrtyd, although a name unfamiliar to outsiders until the late nineteenth century, was for long before that time a favourite place of resort for people from South Wales on high days and holidays. When the fame of the wells had spread and a holiday-maker taking his seat at Euston need not vacate it until he reached Llanwrtyd, the towns of Swansea, Carmarthen, Merthyr and Cardiff still continued to send a great many visitors.

The waters of Llanwrtyd, according to Welsh tradition, were known to the Romans and used by them even before the springs of Aquae Sulis. A very long period of neglect or lack of knowledge followed until a clergyman, the Reverend Theophilus Evans, rediscovered their virtues and published an account of his own 'cure'. He had the chronic complaint of radicated scurvy, almost a leprosy, but after a first trial draught of the sulphurous waters, which gave him back his appetite, he applied them both externally and internally for two months until he was completely cured. Two other chalybeate springs were developed, saline being conveyed to the Pump Room from Builth, but the sulphur spring was held in the highest regard. Its water, the strongest in Wales, contained as much sulphuretted hydrogen per gallon as the Old Sulphur Well at Harrogate, and being impregnated with salts it was more palatable.

When this well had been sealed, in a massive airtight marble pedestal, down to bedrock, the water could be seen in a state of effervescence through a plate-glass disc at the top. The pump, a model of such institutions in its time (but now decayed) served hundreds of late Victorian imbibers, whilst the waters were also conveyed to suites of baths in the chief hotel. Ulcers, chronic gout, sciatica, disorders of the liver and kidneys and Bright's disease were among the complaints for which a properly regulated course of the waters was prescribed and special visits paid to the spa. Those were the days before the National Health Service largely substituted physiotherapy for hydrotherapy and 'taking the waters', and free treatment for costly 'cures'.

At an altitude of about 800 feet in a sheltered valley of the Breconshire Hills, Llanwrtyd drew into its several hotels more than valetudinarian visitors. Visitors to the principal hotel, which resembled a snug country house in its comfort, elegance and refinement, enjoyed the fee simple of the baths but had every encouragement to make it a centre for excursions and sporting activities. The noted trout and salmon stream of the Irfon was at hand, good grouse, partridge and snipe shooting were available on the surrounding hills; the pedestrian was tempted into the moors and wooded valleys of the heart of Wales —to Sugar Loaf (1,276ft), to the Abergwesyn plain (1,100ft), to the various waterfalls and Roman mounds; the botanist into riverside reaches in search of rare flowers and ferns, with which the countryside was then blessed. There were pleasure boats on the lake, a shop selling Welsh woollens, a fine golf course and, in the season, concerts almost every evening in the spa grounds with celebrated Welsh vocalists.

A once well-known novelist, Mrs Lynn Linton, called Llanwrtyd her 'Fountain of Jouvence': 'anyone going to Llanwrtyd and taking more than the mere outsides of things, will get pleasure and profit in equal proportions, healing the body and feeding the mind—as well as purifying the taste jaded with the extravagances of a metropolitan season.' To the tourist of today the minor road from Llanwrtyd along the six exquisitely beautiful miles of the Irfon valley to Abergwesyn is itself ample justification for a visit.

The resort of Llangammarch Wells, only four miles down the valley, consisted of little more than the lake and the Pump House Hotel. The tiny Breconshire village itself had little to distinguish it from so many other Welsh villages. The hotel, however, offered two thousand acres of good shooting, while the triangular lake, flanked by gardens and tennis courts in its extensive grounds, was attractive to those 'jaded brainworkers' who needed peace and quiet rather than excitement. There was a golf course within the hotel estate.

The barium chloride spring here was the chief cause of the spa's popularity: administered both externally and internally it was regarded as of special value in heart complaints. Coupled with the bracing, but sheltered climate—the mean temperature in summer was about two degrees lower than that at Greenwich—and the opportunity to take strolls on paths in the hotel grounds 'graduated to provide resistance exercises', it received glowing tributes. For the 'robust pedestrian' there was Eppynt Mountain (1,560ft) and extensive views or a walk through the woods to Shaky Bridge. It is a useful venue for fell and rock-climbing clubs to date.

Builth Wells, where the river Irfon joins the Wye, is a late seven-teenth-century town—anything earlier was destroyed, in 1691, by a catastrophic fire—with, nowadays, a slightly decayed air. Its cattle market and its medicinal waters have both had prominent shares in its life and livelihood. The waters, chalybeate and sulphur, issued from two sets of springs, Park Wells and Glanne Wells. The former, with the Pump Room, about a mile and a half out of the town, were the more important and were the resort chiefly of local squires and their ladies, until the Younger Pitt's niece, Lady Hester Stanhope, made her visit in 1808 and came to settle at nearby Glan Irfon. Lovely woods surrounded Park Wells: there is still an atmosphere of the 'cure' days as one strolls along the quiet, tree-shaded promenade—Gro Green—from the fine eighteenth-century bridge of six arches. The situation of the town, especially seen from a distance, appeals to those with a taste for the picturesque. The remains of its castle (behind the Lion Hotel)—a stronghold built shortly after the conquest, by William I's half-brother, its squat old church tower, and the rocky summit of Car-neddau Hill in the background, contribute to the effect.

'There was a glamour and enchantment about the first view of the shining slate roofs of Builth and the bridge and the winding reaches of the broad and shining river which even now cling about the place and have never quite been dispelled' (*Diary of Francis Kilvert*, April 1875). Kilvert, who had walked over from Clyro on that first occasion of visiting Builth, records Wordsworth saying that he had met the subject of his poem 'Peter Bell' on the road between Builth and Rhayader. He (Wordsworth) attributed the failure of his sister Dorothy's health and intellect to the long walks that she used to take with him further down the Wye valley, between Llyswen and Llanthony, Wordsworth's opinion being that the stretch of the Wye between Hay and Builth was the finest piece of scenery in South Britain (ie everything south of himself in Grasmere). The early guide-books tend to reinforce that view in recommending the 'thousand lovely bits' between Builth and the Wye's outlet to the Severn to those visitors who have appreciated the 'almost perfect picture' of the town itself set against a winding river and background of lofty hills.

Visitors today come more perhaps for the salmon—in the narrows at Builth Rocks—and trout fishing, for boating on the river or to the annual agricultural show—apart from those whose taste for local history (the town is closely associated with Llewelyn, the last native Prince of Wales, whose cave can be seen at Aberedw), or for sampling the flavour and quaintness of once celebrated resorts, brings them to Builth.

The 'hygienic capital of Wales'—or, in larger claim, 'the Montpellier of Great Britain', Llandrindod Wells, still in business as a spa, also depends on other assets in continuing to attract its many visitors. The myth and mystique of the spa, however, have provided its special distinction.

Springs in the Llandrindod district, known to the Romans as 'Balneae Silures', begin the myth. There are numerous traces of Roman occupation in Llandrindod and the three original springs, sulphur, saline and chalybeate, may have been used even earlier by the Britons. Their medicinal use, of course, is much more recent. People from a neighbouring county seem to have derived benefit from taking the waters from the 'Well in the Cuckoo's Grove' (Ffynon-llwyn-y-gog) and the 'Well of the Blacksmith's Dingle' (Ffynon-cwm-y-gog) in the later part of the seventeenth century: the road from Builth was signposted 'To Ye Wells', at that time a cluster of farmhouses round a common. Rediscovery in about 1736 of the saline spring and also of the sulphur well (at the Pump House) is attributed to a resident, Mrs Jenkins, who effected several 'cures' and brought the place itself to wider notice. Within ten years *A Journey to Llandrindod Wells in Radnorshire* was published in verse by someone who had benefited in recovery of his health. This and items in the *Gentlemen's Magazine* further advanced the budding spa's fame.

A speculator from Shropshire saw his opportunity. About mid-century he built houses, leased others and erected a commodious hotel with tasteful grounds near to the parish church. The trickle of visitors increased to a stream seeking relief from all manner of ailments, so that from Easter until the end of autumn the problem became one of overcrowding. With the added attractions of a racecourse, a ballroom, gambling, and other pastimes, Llandrindod temporarily acquired the reputation of 'a gambling and whoring hell patronised by English gentry'. As a result, however, the Wells's growing popularity received a check: towards the end of the eighteenth century, when the hotel lease had expired, its current, perhaps disillusioned owner had the entire premises razed to the ground. The merit of the waters, fortunately, had been given a more lasting and wider repute by a visiting German physician of some eminence, whose personal cure led him to publish a treatise claiming for them 'good effects so conspicuous that they give place to none in Europe'.

Llandegly, about six miles to the east on a tributary of the Ithon, also had mineral springs, saline, sulphur and chalybeate, and a wellhouse of the sulphur one in a meadow. Although it obtained some reputation, especially for the sulphur, and the waters were much valued as a remedy for the 'falling sickness' (St Tecla's disease), the next and subsequent phases of Llandrindod's development were to dim and finally quench its early lustre. Llandegly Rocks and the seventeenth-century meeting house, in which George Fox may have preached, were the other attractions of this village resort.

Llandrindod's revival began in Regency days. Following the publication of another pamphlet on the well's medicinal properties and the conversion, by the owner of the Pump Room, of a small inn into a large boarding establishment, coupled with the development of adjoining saline and sulphur springs, visitors returned in encouraging numbers. Farmhouses were turned into boarding houses, others were enlarged to provide more accommodation, cottages let their best rooms and the golden harvest began to roll in. The construction of the Central Wales Railway from Craven Arms Junction to Llandovery, completed in 1866, set 'The Wells' finally on the road to its established position as a health and holiday resort. Local landowners offered building sites, lodging houses mushroomed, shopping streets were developed, new medicinal springs were brought to light and the spa began to take its present shape. A population of less than 350 in 1871 rose to 1,624 by 1899, then almost doubled again by 1911, a figure at which it remains today. What had perhaps seemed likely to revert to and remain a place quite out of the region of fashion, quiet, slow and unexciting, became a busy centre, with a dozen or so hotels, ten churches of various denominations, two large public halls, spa 'rinkeries' and a spread of spacious avenues and crescents, attracting an annual total of around 80,000 visitors.

In its fashionable era as a watering-place those who came for the three-week cure to Llandrindod Wells were chiefly sufferers from gout and rheumatism, bronchial affections, dyspepsia, anaemia, insomnia and gravel. The gravel patients came in preference to going to Contreville: those seeking the saline waters came instead of going to Homburg or Kissengen (whose waters were closely similar in analysis). Others were simply fleeing from the metropolis for relief from nervous exhaustion in the combination of mountain air and mild exercise and a mild aperient. The anaemic sought the tonic chalybeate spring, while the sulphur waters, being speedy eliminators of waste products and toxins, had beneficial results on the complex of toxaemias which cause rheumatic and similar conditions. A total of thirty springs provided an unlimited supply of mineral water: a medal awarded at the Balneological Exhibition, Frankfurt, vouched for their quality. Although the National Health Service 'pulled the plug out' of the spa business—when doctors could send their patients off for therapy and other sophisticated treatment free—private treatment is still available here at the Spa Treatment centre.

(Other factors contributing to the decline of the spa idea, as such, have been changes in eating habits, with less gout and liver complaints in their wake, the prevalence of healthier and more active ways of living, greater stringency in middle-class spending and/or more adventurous holiday-making, and also reaction against the old-fashioned style of spa towns and their somewhat pretentious social appeal. One place with chalybeate waters in North Wales, Trefriw, near Llanrwst, a jumbled village with villas and a Victorianised church, known also for its local weaving, finally went out of business around 1933—when the steamer ceased to go up river from Conway.)

Llandrindod Wells stands at an elevation of 700 feet, midway between that of Buxton (1,000ft) and Harrogate (450ft), and is visited by an air neither too keen nor too moist. Well-ventilated, unpolluted by industrial haze, yet mild enough to suit those who come for recuperation, its situation recommends it to many others who come for a visit and in some cases stay to live. Elizabeth Braddon, Victorian novelist of *Lady Audley's Secret* fame, saw fit to celebrate it and its salubrity in one of her books. A well-known modern writer came for a year, thirty or more years ago, and is still there, surrounded by 'the most unspoiled bit of Britain I know'. Llandrindod, in contrast to the little old stone-built towns of Radnorshire, is a 'new town'—'very red-brick, and granddame, very spa, very Malvern, spacious, swept and welcoming'. Its two invaluable assets, clean, healthy air and unchanged beauty of scene, have done much to carry this resort's popularity forward from the fading spa era to that, for which its appearance suits it, of the general holiday centre. Two other circumstances have contributed considerably to the quality of the town's life. Apart from being strategically placed at the crossroads in mid-Wales, it became, from the nineties, a county town in fact, if not in name, so that its garden city style has not been swamped by purely commercial development. The town council has been careful to maintain and enhance its desirable attributes—of common, lake, woodland on the immediate outskirts and a 'recreation' island in the town's midst, facing Rock Park with its Pavilion and Pump Room. And, with its space and facilities, it has also become both a sports championship and conference centre on a national level. To tempt those who come for one reason to stay again for another and explore the area there can be seen from the golf course Sugar Loaf in Carmarthenshire, Montgomery's Kerry Hills and the Black Mountains of Monmouthshire, whilst the quieter hills and lovely wooded valleys of Radnorshire lie just to hand.

So with the bowling events and the eisteddfau, the drama festivals and church assemblies which find their natural 'home' there, it can fairly be said that 'sooner or later everybody in Wales who is anybody can be met in the clean, pleasant streets of Llandrindod Wells'. Or, in contemporary vein, by the Lake Pleasurescope fun centre, 'meet happy people in the heart of singing, swinging Wales'.

Chapter Eight

PICTURESQUE RESORTS

Nature, dear Nature, is my goddess
Whether arrayed in rustic bodice,
Or when the nicest touch of Art
Doth to her charms new charms impart:
But still I, somehow, love her best
When she's in russet mantle drest:
I do not mean in shape grotesque
But when she's truly picturesque.

WILLIAM COMBE, *The First Tour of Dr Syntax*

TRAVELLERS IN England were not, on the whole, until well past mid-eighteenth century, out to see the world aesthetically. John Leland, the first to investigate the English countryside, in 1540, catalogued facts, crops, cattle, buildings; Fynes Morison noticed, in his 1617 Itinerary, inns, forests, fuel and iron mills; Defoe in 1724 made observations on roads, manufactories, manorial estates, products; the reviser of Camden's *Britannia*, 1738, mentioned pleasant 'prospects' from castle or great house, but rather as an appurtenance than anything else. Guidebook writers tended to be bald in style, practical and pedestrian.

Getting about by road, before good turnpikes were laid, was not so easy or pleasant that one journeyed from place to place simply to see the view. Pepys frequently commented on the badness of the ways: 'sometimes we were ready to have our horses sink to the belly' or 'hired a coach to save our own horses'. And when, as recently as the seventeenth century, half of the kingdom had been either moor, forest or fen, the useful aspects of the land and developments in or on it were of greater interest—apart from a few natural wonders like Cheddar or the Peak. Only within the last sixty years, wrote Wordsworth in 1822, did travellers 'instead of confining their observations to towns, manu-factories or mines, begin—a thing till then unheard of—to wander over the island in search of sequestered spots' with 'a relish for the select parts of natural scenery'.

Nature tamed, not wild, had been the traveller's concern so far, but partly because no one had opened his eyes to other aspects. That illumination came chiefly from two travellers, the Reverend William Gilpin and Thomas Pennant. Pennant, a naturalist from Wales, made known the beauties of Scotland in an account of his tour of 1769— it was well known to Silas Neville on his tour a few years later—and also described the approach to the Lakes. Gilpin, native of Cumber-land and Vicar of Boldre in the New Forest, published his observations, made in 1772, on the mountains and lakes of Cumberland and West-morland and on the River Wye, 'relative chiefly to picturesque beauty'. Uvedale Price defined the 'beautiful' as smooth, gentle, of graded colours and textures, the 'picturesque' as rough, asymmetrical, irregular and abruptly various. It was the picturesque that caught on: the sort of scenery that Thomas Gray, writing a *Journal of the Lakes* to a friend (published in 1775), found to be a mixture of 'turbulent chaos of mountain behind mountain, rolled in confusion' and the 'shining purity of the lake, just ruffled by the breeze, reflecting rocks, woods, fields and inverted tops'. Between them Gilpin, Gray and Pennant introduced the Lake District—formerly not considered worth an expensive journey to see—to the public, though not with the avowed intention of turning it into the Englishman's playground, and so virtually founded the tourist movement.

Gray stayed at Keswick: shunned Ambleside, where 'the best bed-chamber was dark and damp as a cellar', gave up Winandermere in despair, and went on, though some parts of the turnpike were not yet made, to an 'old, ill-contrived inn' at Kendal. His dramatisation of 'beauties lying in the lap of Horror', along with the high-priestly, first real guide-book to the Lakes, by the Reverend Thomas West (1778), did much to bring tourists into the district and to turn the new way of looking at Nature into a fashion. West worked out in great detail specially selected viewpoints where the devotee of the picturesque might station himself in order to see 'the delicate touches of Claude verified on Coniston Lake, the noble scenes of Poussin exhibited on Windermere-water or the stupendous romantic ideas of Salvator Rosa realised on the Lake of Derwent'. His *Guide* reached a seventh edition by 1799. But clearly, if the district wanted visitors in greater numbers —and in a countryside where money was scarce and living hard, rich tourists would be as welcome as Father Christmas—development was needed. The visiting of watering places was a relic, though far removed, of the old pilgrimages to holy wells and miracle-working fountains, and there was sometimes residual provision for visitors; but in the pilgrimage to the Lakes, which, as soon appeared, 'it will be considered want of taste not to be able to speak about', a new demand had to be met with both accommodation and amenities.

Keswick, which Wordsworth was already calling the headquarters of tourists, was quick off the mark in amenities and extra attractions. A regatta on Derwentwater was established in the 1780s and boats could be hired from the keeper of the museum. A second museum was set up, and, according to records, visited by over 'fifteen hundred persons of rank and fashion' in 1795. A zig-zag path, constructed by the keeper of this second museum, was made to the top of Latrigg, steps were cut in the rock for visitors to Scale Force and the first beacon was built on Skiddaw, in 1796. The museum did a lively trade also in maps, prints and guide-books. Kendal had a museum too, and Ambleside, early in the nineteenth century, an Exhibition (Green's) of local aquatints and drawings. Ambleside also had its circulating library 'to drive away the ennui which generally pays an unwelcome visit to the fireside on a wet day'. There were booksellers' shops, sports meetings and road widening to take carriages. The *Lonsdale Magazine* for 1820–2 quotes, in its review of Green's 'new and accurate guide', good accommodation now at Ambleside inns, besides genteel lodging at private houses. Reference is made to the New Inn, Coniston for travellers and to boats available there for 'aquatic excursions'; to Low Wood Inn, between Ambleside and Windermere, for the 'exquisite composition' of the views from its bowling green; and to the Ferry

Inn, just across the water from Bowness (now a freshwater biological research station), for the 'station' justly acknowledged to command the noblest view of the lake and its contiguous mountains, 'beauties only unveiled to the disciple of cultivated taste'. As yet there are no respectable villages on the banks of Ullswater 'capable of accommodating the influx of genteel company which crowds to the Lakes during the

Bowness, from Belle Isle, Windermere, from *A Hand-book to the English Lakes*

summer months'. The inn at Patterdale is an 'inferior station' and no post-horses are kept.

These times, after the making of the turnpikes and before the coming of the railways, were the heyday of picturesque travel. It was opportune too for a Briton to appreciate the scenery of his own country and give a boost to his national morale, when most European travel was ruled out by the Napoleonic War. A whole generation of gentlefolk took to the road and set off in search of 'select parts of natural scenery', perhaps with a 'Claude glass' to obtain reflected views. Most of them drove or rode, but sometimes the young nobility and gentry, 'habited like sailors, with knapsacks slung at their backs', gained admission into village bar parlours with difficulty, until they turned out to be as excellent paymasters as they were fastidious guests. An observer in 1817 noted a character change, in the Lakes' inhabitants, as a consequence of the influx, from simple hospitality to commercialism. It is amusing to notice how the veering of taste altered the tone of guide-book writers towards other kinds of scenery. George Lipscombe, in describing a journey to South Wales 1799, cannot omit to remark, apropos the scenery from the top of Malvern, 'that even the windings of the Severn itself, and the famed meads through which it flows, do not compensate for the want of bold and striking scenery. There are no forests, no lakes, no woodland prospects, no rough or boldly projecting eminences, no rocks.' In short, as the pungent parodist of the whole movement was to observe:

> The first, the middle and the last
> In picturesque is bold contrast.
> (*The Tour of Dr Syntax in Search of the Picturesque*
> with illustrations by Thomas Rowlandson, 1812)

—and the absence of it elsewhere than in the environs of Keswick was a disappointment.

The cult, it will be seen, had its own language and imagery. Instead of calling hills steep, one said they were 'bold'; strange, uncouth surfaces became 'irregular and rugged'; distant objects which were out of sight were 'indistinct through the soft medium of a hazy atmosphere'. If a countryside merely united beauty and utility it failed to satisfy: it must be full of rocks and promontories, grey moss and brushwood; its trees must not be straight and flourishing, but crooked, twisted and blasted; its building must not be snug farms, but ruined tattered cottages and watch-towers, surrounded by nettles, thistles and heath blossoms; and, for preference, instead of tidy, happy villagers there should be banditti. As Marianne remarked (*Sense and Sensibility*), 'Admiration of landscape scenery is become a mere jargon. Everybody pretends to feel and tries to describe with the taste and elegance of him who first defined what picturesque beauty was.' She, of course, like her creator Jane Austen, detested jargon of any kind.

In the Lake District above all areas—Wales and the Wye valley

being other favourites—the notion of the picturesque was realisable
in a most compact, varied and exciting form. With and after the fame
of the Lake poets—of whom both Coleridge and Wordsworth
tackled Scafell Pikes—and as the progress of the Industrial Revolution
made periodic retirement from the urban to the sylvan again more and
more desirable, the Lake resorts gradually began to change. Tourists,
no longer pioneers or almost explorers, became holiday-makers: the

Head of Winandermere looking towards Brathay, from *A Hand-book to the
English Lakes*

mysterious fastnesses of the fells and dalehead crossings, such as Sty-
head, were mapped and measured: instead of being known locally as
the 'Devil's chamberpot' and as 'Beauty lying in the lap of Horror',
Derwentwater became the 'Elysium of the North'. The tourist centres
began to acquire a faint resemblance to the spa and seaside resorts,
with 'promenades', rows of boarding houses, fancier shops and new
hotels. Wordsworth had seen fit to object to the obtrusive buildings
put up by visitors 'flocking hither from all parts of England', whose
fancies were smitten so deeply that they became settlers; to the defacing

by 'improvements' of islands on Derwentwater and Winandermere;
to the crowning of naked summits by settlers' houses out of 'craving
for prospect' (one still sees it happening). After the coming of the
railway (a branch of the Lancaster–Carlisle line), it was not merely a
question of isolated buildings, however, but of a whole new town.

Windermere was a railway creation—a direct consequence of the
line's 'rash assault'. Up to that time, 1847, the town of Windermere

Advertisement for lodging house from Poet Close's *Grand Lake Book*

did not exist—only the hamlet Birthwaite, in the township of Apple-
thwaite in the parish of Windermere. Before the railway there was no
village called Windermere and there were no lodging houses nearer
than Bowness. First the station and Rigg's Windermere Hotel opposite
were built, the latter with quite a fine ironwork verandah. Cottages in
Cross Street to the south and a terrace of houses overlooking the
station soon followed, then developments along Victoria Road and

Crescent Road in the direction of Bowness. The atmosphere of gentility that surrounded the station area influenced the total appearance of the town and indicates also the growing democratisation of Lakeland's clientele. Housing on similar lines overtook Bowness, where the White Lion had become the Royal Hotel consequent upon Queen Adelaide's visit in 1840. An industrial magnate of Furness, H. W. Schneider, who had settled at Belsfield House (now Hotel), a vantage point for some of the most picturesque views and graced by a superb Adam ceiling, played the developer's part. Later on ribbon development was to link the two former villages, providing a clear pattern of tourism and holiday resort community, quite different in kind from the pattern and atmosphere of the older market centres, Ambleside, Cockermouth, Keswick and Kendal (capital-to-be of Cumbria). Windermere now ranks as one of England's most important holiday centres, with a wide range of accommodation; Bowness as one of the chief yachting places, centre for water sports and pleasure trips of all kinds on the most sophisticated of the lakes.

Railway enterprise in the area occasioned the building of Furness Abbey Hotel in 1847 (now demolished) and the massive Grange Hotel close by the station, for another 'railway resort'. There was a railway station at the foot of Lake Windermere, 'tastefully constructed of yellow brick, roofed with red tiles', with its refreshment room and adjoining hotel also. When, in 1864, the opening of the Cockermouth–Keswick–Penrith freight line gave a further incentive to tourism, the company built the Keswick Hotel in the hope of monopolising this trade. 'It is connected with the railway station by a covered way; porters attend all the trains and the guests virtually alight at and depart from the hotel . . . Spacious coffee and drawing rooms: a commodious reading room well supplied with books, periodicals and newspapers.' It sounds a little too like station platform accommodation, but, of course, it also commanded 'views of unsurpassed loveliness including the heights of the principal mountains of the district'.

While the railways went all out for tourist traffic—the Furness Railway offered a choice of twenty 'coach and steam yacht tours through Lakeland' daily during the four summer months, with a gondola on Lake Coniston—and guide-books advised on the more picturesque of the rail approach routes, hotels vied with each other in attracting clientele. 'Patronised by the Duke and Duchess of Westminster and several distinguished families, amidst the most romantic scenery in the picturesque Vale of Borrowdale' was one well-tried gambit. Or, at Grasmere 'which is universally admitted to be by far the most lovely spot in the whole Lake District and the most central, whether for carriage or pony track excursions' the Lake Hotel, rebuilt in 1856, 'has enjoyed the patronage of HRH the Prince of Wales and Prince Arthur: boats, mountain ponies and guides'. For taking the

Advertisement for Royal Hotel, Bowness, from Poet Close's *Grand Lake Book*

more adventurous early visitors up Skiddaw or possibly Helvellyn, guides had been attached to the leading hotels, Alpine fashion, in places like Keswick and Ambleside where 'men, loitering about the streets gazing in stationers' windows, for the most part dressed as mountaineers'—as they do today. Not to be outdone the Royal Oak, Keswick, quoted the King of Saxony, a Russian Grand Duke and a Queen Dowager as patrons, while the Queen's struck a balance between distinguished patronage and the contemporary trend by acting as headquarters of the Cyclist Touring Club. Windermere, having it both ways, and asserting its standing as an inland watering place, claimed the only hydropathic in the Lake District, with the largest dining and drawing rooms. (Conishead Priory Hydropathic Mansion, with a Priory omnibus to meet every train at Ulverston, was accessible to, but not in, the Lakes proper.) A handsome, spacious building in the French-Italian style, this Windermere hydro offered 'every convenience for health and pleasure'—massage and pumiline preparations in connexion with Turkish and other baths, a large ballroom and a Ladies' Orchestra. The Old England, Bowness, headquarters of the Royal Windermere Yacht Club—and within a hundred yards of the steamboat pier—was open for the reception of the 'best English and American families'. The Royal, where queens and dukes sojourned, had over 3,000 visitors in the 1868 season.

Despite the cosmopolitan hotels and their snob appeal, and despite also the coming of 'excursion trains' with all that implies, the Lake District was a place of resort chiefly, and congenially, for the nineteenth-century middle class, where, for residence, a good sprinkling of retired clergymen, professors, business men and intellectuals of independent means provided the leavening. Dr Arnold of Rugby, for example, and Matthew Arnold occupied 'Fox How', Rydal. The point of view of the excursionist was put revealingly by *Punch* in 1887:

> At Windermere a party of Excursionists alighted,
> Exulting in their enterprise with pardonable pride:
> The latent poetry within their bosoms was excited,
> Said they, 'We're near our yearned-for beer—we've got to Ambleside.'
>
> 'Excuse me, but you ain't there yet,' observed the Station-master
> (An excellent official, if a trifle cut and dried),
> 'You can reach it in an hour, though you'll have to step out faster,
> Four mile we make it by the lake from here to Ambleside.'
>
> 'We've come out to enjoy ourselves. You don't ketch us a-walkin',
> We ain't such fools as that, no fear, when we've a chance to ride.
> So put us in the train, old chap, and don't stand there a-talkin',
> The terminus for all of us, d'ye see, is Ambleside' . . .
>
> 'Cheer up!' the Station-master said, 'and don't give way to lowness,
> For here are lakes and mountain peaks—a panorama wide:
> From Waterloo to Biscay How, from Newby Bridge to Bowness,
> I think you'll find it ain't behind the view from Ambleside.'

'Our scenery is "picturesque if not precisely eerie",
As you may see it stated in the *Illustrated Guide*':
Said they, 'Them mountains blocks the view, and everythink is dreary,
There must be more to see for sure, out there in Ambleside.'

(By the Very Last of the Lake Poets)

The occasion of this 'Cry from Ambleside'—the attempt to get a
Bill passed to extend the line thither—was not attended with success.
The theory that the best Nature-lover's point of view is a third-class
smoking carriage failed to win the day against the 'sentimental
Ruskinites' and middle-class intellectuals, those who had enough of
comfort and ease elsewhere and preferred to take their stimulus of
mountain air and scenery afoot and in more select company.

By Ruskin's later age, when the Victorian tourist trade was at its
height, the cult of the picturesque had acquired, instead of aesthetic,
moral, almost Sunday-schoolish overtones. Black's *Picturesque Guide
to the Lakes*, with its illustrations by Birket Foster and lavish quotation
from Mrs Hemans, strikes the note. From the mansion of Elleray, near
Windermere village—a house belonging at an earlier date to 'Christopher North' (Professor John Wilson) who anticipated the modern
hiker's enjoyment of the Lake District as a 'gigantic gymnasium' for
climbing, riding, swimming—one reads that 'the scene around is itself
a festival. I never saw any landscape bearing so triumphant a character.
The house, which is beautiful, seems built as if to overlook some fairy
pageant, something like the Venetian splendour of old, on the glorious
lake beneath.' Wilson himself had found the view, up-lake from
Rayrigg, 'one to which there was nothing to compare in the hanging
gardens of Babylon—the widest breadth of water, the richest fore-
ground of wood, the most magnificent background of mountains, not
only in Westmorland, but, believe us, in all the world'. The peaks
visible include the Langdale Pikes, Bowfell, Great End, Great Gable
and Scafell Pike. Apropos another such scene, Mrs Hemans wrote:

Oh! ne'er may man, with touch unhallow'd, jar
The perfect music of the charm serene!
Still, still unchanged, may *one* sweet region wear
Smiles that subdue the soul to love, and tears and prayer!

Windermere

Ambleside, Keswick and Windermere were now well supplied with both old and new hotels, new churches and other amenities. Ambleside built its somewhat uncharacteristic St Mary's with brooch spire (by Gilbert Scott) in 1850-4, its Gothic market house in 1863, its large gabled Prince of Wales Hotel in 1855. St John's, Keswick (where Hugh Walpole was to worship during his *Rogue Herries* period), built in 1838, was much extended in the sixties and eighties. St Mary's, Windermere, was also largely extended, from the original chapel, between the fifties and eighties and various other churches were built there. The hotels were 'alive with elderly ladies, who betrayed an astonishing acquaintance with the names of the mountains, and apportioned them off for successive days as if they were dishes for luncheon and dinner' (William Black: *The Strange Adventures of a Phaeton*, 1874).

Windermere, as a contemporary guide remarks, was 'the little town of new villas, new church, new collegiate institution (Wordsworth College), new streets and new and commodious hotel—in every respect and to all classes a most pleasant resting place'. A visitor who had known Windermere as a girl, was quite bewildered by the 'new buildings and the cuttings of terraces and alteration of gardens, the houses that had sprung up of late years', and could hardly find the way again to Elleray (William Black). Its advantage over all the other lake villages was its elevation, just under Orrest Head with its splendid panoramic views.

Apart, however, from such older buildings of character as Keswick's eye-catching Moot Hall (1813), the resort centres have no special pretensions architecturally: the natural architecture of the district makes up for it, with its rock pillars and buttresses, its precipices and the 'gorgeous pavilions' of its fells.

Ruskin's fear, however, amid all this, that the opening of a railway extension would lead to the opening of 'tavern and skittle grounds round Grasmere, which will soon then be nothing but a pool of drainage, with a beach of broken ginger-beer bottles, [where] operatives' minds will be no more improved by contemplating the scenery than of Blackpool' was not realised—yet. Visitors to the hotels used their private horse buses, open and closed carriages, horse charabancs or four-in-hands from and to the railway stations, to the steam yacht piers and to get about the district. The comicality, amid such scenery, of the men's jackets and resplendent knickerbockers 'such as would have made a harlequin blush', with their young ladies 'tarred and feathered as it were with staring stripes and alarming petticoats and sailors' hats of straw', did not pass without comment. 'Why should the borders of a lake be provocative of these mad eccentricities?' But, it was concluded, they were quite harmless. The real threat of turning Lakeland resorts into miniature Blackpools was foreshadowed only in the early decades of the twentieth century. Then, alongside the four-in-hands, hotels began to advertise 'motor charabancs leave this hotel daily to all parts of the Lake District'; to carry brochures for the 'Inimitable tours in powerful private motor cars' offered by new companies; or even to put forward, with their electric lights and modern sanitation, 'covered garage, inspection pit, charging and vulcanising'. The Ullswater Royal Mail, pioneers of the direct motor service, had by the twenties linked Penrith with Patterdale all the year round.

When the small car became popular and when, later, the touring caravan idea took hold, those who, in Wordsworth's phrase 'wandered over the island in search of sequestered spots', found the Lake District in season the reverse of 'lonely as a cloud'. Signs of conflict, between hoteliers' and boarding-house keepers' and tradesmen's desire to encourage more and more visitors and the wish of the conservationists and Friends of the Lake District to maintain what the current postal overprint for this area terms 'the roots of heaven' in that earthly near-perfect state are everywhere conspicuous today. To find a place for carparks, caravan parks, camp-sites, picnic spots, steak-bars, boutiques, speedboats, even noisy power-boat contests, in an area whose natural attractions are diminished by them or their close proximity, is an increasing problem. If one accepts that between the waterfronts at Bowness and at Blackpool, on a fine day of national holiday, the chief difference is one of size and degree, where does the tourist-trap and stall-setting outlook stop? Even tradespeople do not want to kill the goose that lays the golden eggs: Cumberland's and Westmorland's economy needs its tourist Father Christmas. Yet even the fell-walkers' remote footpaths and shepherds' tracks have become, especially since the publication of a series of closely detailed and do-it-yourself

pedestrian/scrambler guide-books, more like drovers' roads, where all
and sundry help to blaze the trial with litter.

The position lends itself to exaggeration, as it has done almost from
the beginning of the picturesque cult. Off season, when there is neither
a convention, a regatta, sports nor an opera (at Rosehill—the northern
Glyndbourne—near Whitehaven), the lakeland resorts still preserve
much of the atmosphere of their early nineteenth-century and Victorian origin. In some the 'pace slackens to the nostalgic atmosphere of
the late-Victorian spa'. Unable to escape from it, boarding houses at
Windermere capitalise on the Victorianism, while a hotel at Bowness
even has its bedroom washbasins set into the old marble-topped
Victorian stands. Grasmere keeps its Victorian home-made ginger-
bread shop and some of its Victorian lodges and cottages. When the
sports are over and all the curio and craft shops, the perfumery and
picture galleries, postcard stalls and snack-bars closed or quiescent
and the modernised hotels with their Scandinavian lay-out largely
denuded, the sense of changelessness returns to the solid buildings of
Westmorland slate or white-washed stone, with their great rounded
chimneys, mature timber or vast rhododendron shrubberies and
mountain backcloth. The crowded and noisy summer is forgotten.
Ambleside, too, town of grey slate houses and grey slate roofs, irregular streets with steep pitches or archway descents, of old watermill
and miniature bridge cottage, seems to retire into its past. Keswick,
apart from its boarding houses, half becomes again the 'dull manu-
facturing town, neither picturesque nor beautiful, but with a charming smell of cedar pencils' that Coleridge and Southey knew. The
lakes, too, come into their own again: Windermere in its elegant,
rather formal beauty, Coniston's wooded length dominated by the
Old Man, the Italianate loveliness of Derwentwater.

Even on a Bank Holiday one can find a quiet corner, perhaps half
a mile away from the tourist tracks, and, as the *Tourist Board Magazine*
claims, 'dream away a long afternoon without seeing another human
being'. For those, that is, with imagination and initiative, the claim is
valid. A survey undertaken by the National Parks Commission and the
BTA in 1967 calculated a total of 50,400 visitors to the district on an
August Sunday, of whom about one quarter were day or half-day

visitors, less than one sixth of these coming to walk. Of the rest, staying for the weekend or longer, nearly half were there to walk or climb. The longer stayers would be more likely to succeed in avoiding the beaten track. But even rock-climbers are beginning to complain that in a popular valley like Langdale, on a popular crag such as Gimmer, an August Sunday may see two hundred or more of them 'in the queue' for routes, whilst on a campsite suitable for three hundred at most, nearly twice that number have been known to descend for tent-space. Now that the M6 motorway is completed, the Lake District's problem, to remain popular and peaceful enough for the 'picturesque traveller', is still more acute. Ruskin's adjuration to engineers and contractors, to withhold from 'making a steam merry-go-round of the Lake country' is as necessary as ever.

Of the other places which attracted the picturesque traveller Wales also owed a good deal initially to Thomas Pennant. A native of Mostyn, Flint, he produced his *Tour in Wales* in 1778, at a time when coach travel was making it possible for cultivated Englishmen, with an interest in scenery and antiquities, to go further afield. In the north both Wordsworth and Sir Walter Scott paid attention to Llangollen, visiting the 'Ladies of Llangollen'—two unmarried Irishwomen of title who had romantically settled there. Later visitors had the commendations of George Borrow (*Wild Wales*, 1862) and Ruskin as added afflatus to the Vale's natural attractions. 'One of the most beautiful and delightful little towns in Wales or anywhere else,' pronounced Ruskin. From their day on, tourists have continued to make a beeline for the Vale of Llangollen. 'If you are seeking peace and scenic charm avoid the first week in July' warns a hotel guide: 'the International Eisteddfod fills every bed for miles around.' And if you care about atmosphere, one might add, rather than comfort and convenience, turn a blind eye to the extensive rebuilding in the town itself, carried out in glazed brick.

Betws-y-coed was a smaller enchanter, before it became too touristy and celebrated. David Cox, who initiated its fame as a beauty spot after his tour of North Wales in 1805–6, painted the sign for one of the old-established inns. Towards the end of the century the inn's proprietor ran four-horse coaches daily through the passes of Llanberis,

Gwynant and Aberglaslyn, and to Beddgelert and Snowdonia. Visitors to this unrivalled centre for the scenery of North Wales were transported by private road in the proprietor's omnibus to and from the station and to such sights as the Swallow Falls.

Dolgelley was considered by Thomas Love Peacock as one of the most beautiful of places; Thackeray also noticed Dolgelley:

> If ever you come to Dolgellau
> Don't stay at the —— Hotel.
> There's nothing to put in your belly
> And no one to answer the bell.

Later the Cambrian Railways published an official guide, *Picturesque Wales*, to encourage first-, second- and third-class travellers to sample the delights of Dolgelley, Bala, Ffestiniog slate quarries, Rhayader and the valley of the Wye, as well as the coastal resorts. 'The scenery adjacent to and traversed by the Cambrian railways is of an exceedingly varied and beautiful description . . . special tickets at reduced fares between local stations to tourist, pic-nic and other parties.' The GWR also lured the tourist to both North and South Wales with the additional feature of 'family carriages (with lavatories and other conveniences) containing compartments for servants', on payment of not less than four first-class and four second-class fares. Not to be outdone, in this view-bagging age, the Midland line from London to Liverpool made capital out of *its* picturesque route through the vale of the Derwent, Matlock and the Peak of Derbyshire and offered 'drawing room saloon cars', in which refreshments were served, on its day expresses.

In South Wales, Abergavenny—home of Squire Bramble in *Humphrey Clinker*—established itself as a picturesque tourist centre, with the distinctive landmark of Sugar Loaf Hill and proximity to the Black Mountains and Brecon Beacons. Salmon and trout fishing, charming roads for cycling or driving to Llanthony Abbey, Crickowell and Raglan added their attractions. Henry James was a visitor to Abergavenny, climbing the hills and admiring the primroses. Brecon, a place favoured by the well-to-do, proclaims itself the most convenient inland centre in Wales. It has associations with Mrs Siddons and her brother Charles Kemble, who lived at 47 High Street, and, earlier, with the antiquarian John Aubrey. The Captain's Walk was a favourite lounge there during the Napoleonic Wars: there is a classical style Shire Hall (1842), and the Bulwark—which all have helped to set the tone.

It is interesting to note that the 'tourist nuisance' was already felt by sensitive residents and neighbours of popular visiting places even a hundred years ago. 'About a mile above Llanthony we described the Abbey ruins,* the dim grey pile of building in the vale below standing by the little riverside among its brilliant green meadows. What was our horror on entering the enclosure to see two tourists with staves and shoulder belts all complete postured among the ruins in an attitude of admiration, one of them of course discoursing learnedly to his gaping companion and pointing out objects of interest with his stick. If there is one thing more hateful than another it is being told what to admire and having objects pointed out to one with a stick. Of all noxious animals too the most noxious is a tourist. And of all tourists the most vulgar, illbred, offensive and loathsome is the British tourist' (*Kilvert's Diary*: 1870). Sixty years later, guide-books to 'unbeaten tracks' for hikers were coming out, since it was 'certainly only along her by-ways and unbeaten tracks that nowadays [could] be found England's unsullied beauties and unsmirched charms'!

A concern of all popular picturesque resorts is to avoid the dangers of reaching saturation point, attendant on the increase of population, affluence, leisure and cars. Whereas tourism contributes to the conservation of the countryside *for* public enjoyment and to the preservation within it of ancient monuments, villages, inns and other attractive buildings, since without visitors such places might have insufficient traffic to justify their maintenance, the need to protect beauty spots *from* the public arises when such traffic becomes excessive. A recent proposal to ban all motor vehicles, save those serving local households, from Langdale in the summer season, is one example of this type of protection; or to divert from the centre to the perimeter of the district those who come chiefly to camp, by providing a site with special attractions at the southern end of Lake Windermere. More

* The ruins belonged to Walter Savage Landor.

acceptable in most cases would be extension of the visiting season, coupled with improved access and movement within the area, so that visitors could be dispersed more evenly across it in both space and time. For, as one tea-room proprietor said, of visitors to Grasmere, 'You could walk on their heads almost in summer'. It is not sufficient to conserve breath-taking views across open landscape, by avoiding the introduction of discordant artefacts, buildings and arterial roads, if tourists themselves and the provision for their needs swamp that which they come to see.

'The panorama over dale and mountain showed no scars, there was neither noise, nor fumes, nor litter, nor the noise of aircraft' (Friends of the Lake District: *News Letter*, June 1971). Of how many places, excluding this carefully chosen section of a National Park, can that still be said? And in twenty or thirty years hence?

Chapter Nine

HEATH AND
FOREST CENTRES

As WILL already be obvious, a number of resorts such as Ilkley, Shap, Llandrindod, Woodhall Spa and Buxton did not rely solely on their waters to bring in the golden harvest, but also advertised the heather moors or woodland charm of their respective localities. This ingredient of the retired, healthy holiday place was also exploited independently in the nineteenth century and quite apart from the cult of the 'picturesque'.

Lyndhurst, capital of the New Forest, provides a conspicuous example of the source of appeal. The original forest, called 'Stene' (land of the Jutes) up to 1100, once stretched from the border of Wiltshire to the south coast, from the river Avon to Southampton, and was of oak; later plantations were of beech, to make up the loss by illegal felling over the centuries, and in Victorian times largely of fir. The 'forest', of course, is not merely a huge, ancient wood—covering even today over 92,000 acres—but a richly varied countryside of streams, ponds, heath and moorland, with old earthworks and barrows and sequestered thatched villages among the bracken. Wild deer, forest ponies—some 3,000 of them—rare birds, moths and other insects make their homes here. In short, it seems like a bit of old England and the 'wild'. The fact that in the northern and wildest part William Rufus was killed by an arrow adds its historical 'romance'.

The healthy scents of pine and gorse instead of acrid smoke, the silent glades of beech and oak instead of crowded streets and mews, the unspoilt villages and roaming herds of deer, brought to Lyndhurst the Victorian seeker after nature and solitude and select interests. Poets and artists and musicians came to stay there: Tennyson and William Allingham had already roamed among the great beeches and bracken; Lord Leighton and Hamilton Aide shared their enthusiasm. Other visitors followed to enjoy 'the finest woodland scenery in Europe'. Although Lyndhurst was 'lost in the forest', the railway station was only three miles away and fast trains ran frequently from Waterloo.

To accommodate the influx the large Crown Hotel was rebuilt, in 1897, in an appropriately half-timbered style. Apart from the gabled seventeenth-century Queen's House (where the verderers who administer the forest still meet), most of the other buildings are unremarkable two-storey houses and shops, but the place has its distinctive, unconventional air. A most striking Victorian-Gothic church, of red and yellow brick, including the 160-foot spire, soars above the single street. Leighton painted an altar fresco for it, adding to the interest of its Pre-Raphaelite stained glass and interior columns of Purbeck stone, their capitals carved with leaves of the New Forest trees. Although with the proliferation of motor cars and guest houses the sense of comparative seclusion at Lyndhurst has gone, its appeal remains strong. After all one of the nearby villages, Cadnam, is nowadays the first place where a motorist travelling from London on the A31 can pull off the road into natural forest.

With Brockenhurst (meaning Badger's Wood), formerly a residential village, a few miles to the south, the New Forest capital serves as centre for visiting many other pleasant places. 'What more perfect English setting could one awaken to than the vista, from most of the bedrooms, of New Forest ponies, a lone donkey, flora and fauna blending with century-old trees: by road it is admirably suited for sight-seeing, for within a 25-mile radius, history and loveliness blend' (hotel publicity). Among the pleasant places are Boldre, once home of William Gilpin, pioneer of the picturesque; Sway, where Captain Marryat placed the setting for his *Children of the New Forest*; Burley, with its ancient earthwork on Castle Hill; Beaulieu Heath, with one of Hampshire's few

THE FINEST WOODLAND SCENERY IN EUROPE.

The Crown Hotel, Lyndhurst,

IN THE CENTRE OF THE

NEW FOREST.

3 miles from Lyndhurst Road Station, **L. & S.W.R.**

FAST TRAINS RUN FREQUENTLY FROM WATERLOO.

The **ISLE OF WIGHT, BOURNEMOUTH, SOUTHAMPTON,** are
easily accessible from Lyndhurst.

OMNIBUSES MEET ALL TRAINS.
CARRIAGES SENT TO ORDER.

Advertisement from *Tourist's Guide to Somersetshire* by R. N. Worth inland lakes—Hatchet Pond; and nearby Buckler's Hard, famous ship-yard of Nelson's day) and Minstead, an unspoilt village with a church whose family box-pews have their own fire-places. Those who wish to see the whole area ascend Bramble Hill (414ft) north-west of Lynd-hurst; those seeking the biggest oak in the whole forest go to Knight-wood, to the south-west. Some of the biggest beeches are at Mark Ash; but where the tallest Douglas fir is, among the miles and miles of Victorian plantings, is left to conjecture. (A specimen at Powys Castle reaches the height of 170 feet.) One other site in Lyndhurst itself calls for notice by Victorian enthusiasts—the grave of Alice Liddell, original of *Alice in Wonderland*; in Brockenhurst churchyard another celebrated grave can be seen, that of 'Brusher' Mills, snake-catcher.

Epping Forest attracted those Londoners who wanted a taste of the 'wild' more easily accessible than the New Forest or a contrast to Hampstead Heath, favourite place for views over the Home counties. Its extent, in the eighteenth century, was about 60,000 acres, probably only half its size in Elizabethan times, but a tenfold increase over the present acreage. When Pepys journeyed on horseback from Epping into London, through the forest, in 1659, he found the way good enough 'but only in one path which we kept as if we had rode through a kennel [gutter] all the way'. A century or so later Silas Neville found that part of the forest nearest town the pleasantest, and dined on several occasions at the Crown in Epping. The forest was a notorious spot for highwaymen, and on one journey he just missed being at the scene when some gentleman in a carriage, stopped by two of them, shot down one and wounded the other so seriously that he was appre-hended. In Neville's day there were prospects from Epping Place and Coppedhall over great parts of the forest, 'richly diversified with villas, plantations and parks of every description from the palace at Wanstead to a small but neat box of the retired East India captain'. Woodford and Snaresbrook were then pleasing villages on the forest, with their small pieces of water, many capital houses commanding delightful prospects and very rural for a situation so near town.

As Neville was much pleased with the forest views, so have been many others since, including writers, painters and sculptors from Tennyson, who lived in his early poetic days of fame at High Beech, to Sir Jacob Epstein. The forest became public in 1882 and still contains woodland as lovely as any in England, though the A11, which cut the Forest in two, more than halved its magic. To naturalists its hornbeams are of special note—formerly flourishing in much greater numbers in the forest round London and valued for their charcoal used in the making of gunpowder—and also the ferns. A medical herbalist, who called himself 'Old Dido', one of the relics of mountebank quacks, used to offer a chilblain remedy prepared from some mysterious fern, which grew only in the forest. He gained local renown for his cures, treating also backache, whooping cough, measles, liver disorders and burns. As with the spas, the forest resorts attracted their 'empiricks' and oddities. 'Every watering-place has its characters, a class of persons who receive a pseudo-distinction from sundry eccentricities, half humorous sayings, doggerel rhymes etc. . . . and (usually) contrive to eke out a livelihood thereby' (Charles Roger, FSA: *A Week at the Bridge of Allan*).

Drawn & Eng^d by W. Banks Edin^r

The Bridge of Allan, from *A Week at the Bridge of Allan* by Charles Roger

Other Epping features were the so-called Catacombs—an underground grotto built of vast blocks of stone during the nineteenth century—and the genuine iron-age earthworks, marking the site of ancient encampments at Loughton and Ambresbury Banks, 2 miles south-east of Epping. For arboriphiles King's Oak could be added to the list of celebrated veterans, including Knightwood Oak (New Forest), Gospel Oak (Polstead Park), Hawkhurst Oak (Kent), Sidney's Oak at Penshurst, Abbot's Oak (Woburn), the husk of Parliament Oak

(Sherwood Forest), Cowthorpe Oak (near Wetherby) and Ellerslie Oak (Paisley). Fairlop Oak, a thousand-year-old celebrity of Hainault Forest, fell in 1820.

Although the metropolitan octopus threatens so nearly, the market town of Epping, mainly one broad mile-long street with a number of seventeenth-century timbered and plastered houses, still retains separate identity, though accommodating to modern needs One of its old inns has become a 'motel', with public rooms set round a central courtyard and private rooms at the rear to muffle the noise of passing traffic. Another on the edge of the forest, 'two miles only from the Underground Central line', invites guests to eat and sleep 'in seemingly the heart of the country' with their cars parked underneath their windows. But how long will it last with Ringway 3, linking outgoing motorways, already scheduled to skirt the forest's northern edge?

Two less obvious small resorts, deep in the country and attractive to those with selective tastes, Liphook in Hampshire and Dulverton in Somerset, were both also patronised by Tennyson, who seems to have been the accepted arbiter of southern rural attractions, as Wordsworth was of northern. Liphook claims to be a health resort by reason of its salubrious air and pure water, and is near the outskirts of Woolmer Forest. Lord Nelson, Queen Victoria and General Blucher stayed, on their separate occasions, at its seventeenth-century posting inn. Its situation on the Portsmouth road has kept it firmly in the public eye and favour, and also its proximity to the National Trust properties of woodland and heath at Haslemere and Hindhead.

For the discerning, Liphook's situation in a countryside associated both with Tennyson and with Gilbert White adds considerably to the incentive for an extended stay. Selborne, the vicarage home of White, and for that reason one of Hampshire's most famous villages, is only a few miles off. There is the steep, beech-covered chalk hill called the 'Hanger', classically described in all its ways and moods, its bird and animal life, by the eighteenth-century naturalist; there is White's house, the 'Wakes', now containing a museum personal to him and also mementoes of Captain Oates, companion of Scott to the South Pole. The stone-built village gathered round a green or square, the 'Plestor', has an unobtrusive, unspoiled charm; an evening stroll along Short and

Long Lyth is delightful; for the lover of woodland and open spaces, there is the common, including Selborne Hill, also belonging to the National Trust. When Richard Jefferies wrote the preface to the Camelot edition of *The Natural History of Selborne* (first published in 1788 and written in the form of letters to Thomas Pennant), he remarked: 'They say the place is very much the same as when he [White] was there a hundred years ago, for the country changes very slowly: the people, too, move slow, and their memories linger long—memories never seem to die out: those who follow the studies of Mr White out-of-doors will find very little altered and can take up the picture as he left it, and begin to fill in the endless touches which make nature.' Allowing for a few additions and amenities the same might almost be said today and is a large part of the charm by which visitors to Selborne are often induced to return.

Dulverton, general headquarters for the south-eastern part of Exmoor Forest, has a tradition that goes back to the middle ages and a splendid situation between steep wooded hillsides near the junction of two rivers, the Exe and the Barle. One of its hotels, where Tennyson stayed in June 1891, was built in 1873, four years after the publication of Richard Blackmore's popular classic *Lorna Doone*. Since then that 'romance of Exmoor' has helped to bring a constant stream of visitors, besides the huntsman and angler, to a comparatively secluded Somerset township. The salmon and trout fisherman, the stag and fox-hunter, of course, are in first-class country for their pursuits, but as many again come to pursue, with camera or sketch-book, the fleeting impressions of sunlight on water by the prehistoric clapper bridge, Tarr Steps, or over the Barle valley to the hills beyond. From here, as from Simonsbath on the upper reaches of the Barle, there is special inducement—and bracing air—to explore the surrounding countryside, either 'hacking' on an Exmoor pony or walking, instead of motoring. The guest houses emphasise their peace and seclusion, with their shelves full of books and the absence of TV, their log fires and drying rooms, adjacent to or in the midst of the 'walker's paradise' of Exmoor National Park. This 'romantic' district seems to have been given a perennial afflatus by the inclusion in it of the 'Doone Valley' and its association with all those stirring events which Blackmore (himself a Berkshire man) set afoot amid such beautiful descriptions of Exmoor scenery. Probably, in fact, for identification of a particular wild, natural scene with one particular work of fiction, Exmoor stands next only in popular appeal to the Haworth Moors of *Wuthering Heights*—to which almost every Continental and trans-Atlantic visitor is magnetically attracted.

If one had to name the single outstanding characteristic of the British landscape as a whole, it would be difficult to find an answer

Abbey Craig and Ochil Mountains, from *A Week at the Bridge of Allan* by Charles Roger

more appropriate than 'trees', even allowing for the fact that in the highlands of Scotland the answer would have to be 'heather'. Although the word 'forest' does not in its original use signify trees, but only wild country where game is not enclosed—'a district wholly or chiefly devoted to the purposes of the chase', the views of England where one can enjoy the illusion of looking over endless woodland are very often associated with ancient forest names. In this sense Exmoor Forest is not 'characteristic', composed as it is of heather, oak coppices, valleys with lonely thorn trees, bog and open moorland—nor is Charnwood Forest, Leicestershire, although it is said that formerly a man could walk from Bardon Hill to Beaumanor without once seeing the sky. One goes, for the illusion of trees clothing a whole landscape, to Leith Hill, near

Dorking, and looks towards the South Downs across the Weald ('open forest land'); to an elevated part of Tunbridge Wells for more distant, but magnificent views of Ashdown Forest; or to Stinchcombe Hill, near Stroud, to look over the Severn Valley and into the Forest of Dean. Burnham Beeches, Bucks, Wychwood Forest, Oxfordshire and Savernake Forest of elm, beech and oak, Wiltshire, are the extensive woodland remains of historic tracts of 'wild' England.

The areas just mentioned offer favourite places for outings, but they have not seen the development, from such a nucleus as Lyndhurst, of any comparable holiday resorts. Perhaps the area most capable of providing this development is the Forest of Dean, one of the greatest primeval forests in Britain. Raleigh and Drake came here to buy timber for the Fleet—at a time when the royal forest reserves had gone down to 350,000 trees. Pepys, surveying the disposition of the forest in Speede's maps, drew up an agreement for obtaining its timber—accounted the toughest in England—and conveying it from Lydney to Woolwich shipyards. Said now to contain over twenty million trees and some two thousand miles of woodland paths ideal for the walker, the forest has also several little towns and villages—apart from rather ugly Cinderford and plain Coleford, the 'capital'—with the characteristic reticent attractiveness of forest places. St Briavels is perhaps the favourite place of call for visitors. High above a wooded valley which drops down to the Wye, it has the remains of a thirteenth-century castle and a restored Norman church. A native of St Briavels who has worked in a mine for one year and one day is, by custom, a 'free miner' with his own mining right within the forest—this privilege being a reward for Dean miners' services in siege work during the medieval Scottish wars. There are also literary associations, on the northern outskirts of the forest: beyond Gorsley Common and Four Oaks, near Dymock, the American poet Robert Frost lived from 1912 to 1914 and there gathered round him, at one time or another, Edward Thomas, Wilfrid Gibson, John Masefield, John Drinkwater and Rupert Brooke.

Those, then, who seek trees instead of waters for their nature cure, who enjoy the savour of border country or 'Georgian' place-mood, may find here a new stimulus for combining health with pleasure.

Chapter Ten

INLAND RESORTS TODAY: A GAZETTEER

A WHOLE phase of English life lies behind the facades of terrace, pump room, crescent, parade and assembly rooms in the inland watering place. The major resorts, as will have appeared, were deliberately created as setting for a cultured and civilised life of leisure. From Bath, fountain of medicine and manners, to Shap, 'modern' monastery of the spirit under strain, standards of taste obtained to which later generations have become less and less accustomed. Not only were such places, with their tasteful promenades, laid out for the benefit of visitors, oases of rest and recreation, in the original sense; as often as not they have remained, amid the cement deserts of conurbation and the arid wastes of subtopia, oases of greenery and culture. A legacy of fine architecture and fine planning, of small provincial towns blossoming anew with classical buildings and dignified layout, has somehow been largely preserved—though not everywhere alike—and itself still is a means of preserving traditions of cultivated taste and amusement wedded to art. While the picturesque resorts offer natural scenery at its least spoiled and most varied, the spa towns offer man's own created environment at its most seemly and least debased. It should cause no surprise that in the works of the present Poet Laureate, a proud Englishman, evocations of Leamington, Cheltenham, Bath, Matlock, Grasmere, Ambleside, Harrogate and Woodhall Spa occur hardly less frequently than of his favourite Cornwall or Oxford.

148

In reviewing here, briefly, the whole conspectus of resorts, it would be tedious and superfluous to particularise all the cultural activities for which they provide a focus. To older traditions, such as the Drama Festival at Malvern (begun 1929) or the Music Festivals at Bath and Cheltenham, new ones such as the Harrogate Festival of Arts and Sciences or the Lake District Music Festival (begun in 1972) are being added. Integration of setting and performance make for outstanding artistic enjoyment at these festivals: music played in abbey, pump room, guildhall or period assembly room acquires a new dimension, not least when to the departing audience the whole place adds a coda of gracious townscape or natural beauty. Organisers of the Lakes Festival emphasise the especially appropriate conjunction of English Lakeland in spring with the music of Mozart, Haydn, Schumann, Handel, Ravel—'festive music and natural grandeur blended in perfect harmony'.

For the visitor, keen or curious to see what is added by the setting, from those repositories of taste and moulds of a whole phase of English life, the inland resorts themselves, an alphabetically arranged résumé of the more notable has been added. Scottish resorts, which qualified as inland watering places, are also included: to discriminate between the picturesque claims of others, Lowland or Highland, would be too invidious. For this it may be offered in defence that, in Baddeley's opinion, 'in the combinations which constitute scenery as opposed to the powerful presentment of one or two kinds (glen and coast) Scotland must yield the palm to the similar regions of the sister country: Scotland can no more produce a rival to the view of Windermere from the Troutbeck road, or of the Mawddach estuary from Barmouth Bridge, than can England or Wales show anything to vie with the Coolin Hills, Loch Linnhe or Glen Affric.'

GAZETTEER

Ambleside, Westmorland, hub of the Lake District for fell walkers, climbers and seasonal tourists, lies at the head of Lake Windermere. Built on a lower ledge of Wansfell, on the border of a well-wooded valley, it has steep, narrow lanes, and sideroads (including that to the Kirkstone Pass) leading out of a tilted white-and-grey square, over-looked by a market-hall-turned-restaurant. Fairfield and Helvellyn are close and there are good bus services to other places for starting climbs or fell walks. The shops provide all necessary supplies and equipment, camping, weather-proof, photographic, footwear, as well as books, old and new, for the not infrequent wet days. There is a small cinema and an Arts Centre and a superior type youth hostel. Bridge House, north-west of the square, is a curiosity.

Hotels and boarding houses, curio and craft displays abound. When the church, rebuilt in 1812, became too small to accommodate the summer influx, St Mary's was erected (1854). It has a stained glass window in memory of William Wordsworth, presented by his English and American admirers; another window commemorates Matthew Arnold. The traditional rush-bearing ceremony (see under GRASMERE) takes place here, on the last Saturday in July, nearest to St Ann's Day; sports are held in this month also. Seen from Waterhead side in winter, with snow on summits that end-block the main street, Ambleside has a slightly Austrian air and is quite impressive. In summer it can scarcely be seen for the crowds.

The Lake District Festival, in the first fortnight of May, takes various churches, schools and halls at Ambleside, Cartmel, Kendal, Keswick and Windermere for its series of lectures, recitals, films and dancing displays. It also includes conducted tours of National Trust properties with departures from Ambleside and Bowness.

Ballater, Aberdeenshire, has beside it Pannonich Wells, and was first put on the map, literally, in 1760 when an old woman was cured of scrofula by bathing in a bog pool there. At that time the plain on which Ballater stands was bleak moorland without a single house. The publicity given to the cure by Jacobite Colonel Farquharson, who had an inn built, created a fashionable spa around the chalybeate waters, with accommodation at first in nearby hamlets, then in the new village that he founded around 1790. A hundred years ago Ballater comprised groups of villas and cottages clustered round a green, with a graceful spire of the Established Church in the middle, and everything still wore a new look. A wooden bridge then crossed the Dee, instead of the original one swept away by floods in 1829, but the railway station was there and the place seemed 'in high favour and capable of great extension', standing as it does at the entrance to the whole lovely upper valley of Deeside.

Since Queen Victoria had started her visits to Balmoral in 1848, Ballater, of course, was no ordinary station. (She also visited Pannonich, still flourishing in 1870: now, a century later, one can sample the waters at Pannonich Wells Hotel.) The town continues to rank high as a Highland resort on its own merits. It is dry and bracing, sheltered from north winds, but open to soft southerly ones; it has a good golf course, tennis courts and bowling greens; the Victoria Hall for public entertainments; good shops—many bearing the Royal Arms in token of their services to Balmoral—and a good range of accommodation in hotel and boarding house. Ideal for fishing, climbing, hill-walking and pony-trekking in summer, ski-ing in winter, it has also the universal attraction of highland games (begun in 1864), usually held on the third Thursday in August. Apart from the chance of seeing Royalty, sometimes informally, and the grounds of Balmoral (erected by the Prince Consort 1854), tourists find in such features as Knock Castle, Abergeldie Castle and the ancient island site of Castle Kinord or in the view from the summit of Lochnagar (3,786ft) with its crags 'wild and majestic' that Byron 'sighed for', all within close, if not easy reach, ample reason for making their centre Ballater. The highland way of life and hospitality may even convert them into regular visitors.

Bath, Somerset, the re-created Roman city of square, crescent and circus, is for many visitors, especially Continental, the supreme inland resort, *the* city of display and elegance. Its hot springs, Aquae Sulis, in a valley between great hills, were the basis of a Roman pleasure town. The Roman baths remain: around them today is the eighteenth-century pleasure town shaped by the genius of British architects from local stone.

The old Roman elements to see are the Great Bath, 80 feet by 40 feet, open to the sky, its floor covered with the original Mendip lead; the circular bath adjacent, possibly used by women and children; the hypocaust and its mosaic pavement and part of the Roman conduit. In the adjoining museum there is a model of the whole lay-out of the Roman remains stripped of their modern superstructure and many relics, rings, seals, dice and other objects, found on the site. In the place of honour stands a bronze head of Sul Minerva, discovered in 1727, one of the finest extant Roman bronzes.

Bath Abbey, close by, provides a link with the Saxons who destroyed the Roman city in 577. In the original Saxon abbey Edgar was crowned King of England in 973 AD. A great Norman minster, built on the site, was destroyed by fire in 1137 except for an arch to be seen in the present south choir aisle, and the existing abbey was founded in 1499. The carving on the west front represents the founder, Bishop King's, dream of angels ascending and descending a ladder from heaven. Queen Elizabeth I worshipped here in August 1574, and the internal walls are literally covered with memorial tablets of famous Englishmen. (The information bureau near the abbey has a list of those who lived in Bath and of their residences.)

The glories of eighteenth-century Bath are in Queen's Square and the Circus (linked by Gay Street) by John Wood the Elder; in the Royal Crescent (linked to the Circus by Brock Street) and Bath Assembly Rooms (bombed in 1942, restored and decorated by Oliver Messel) by John Wood the Younger; in the Florentine shop-lined Pulteney Bridge by Robert Adam; in Pulteney Street, the Guildhall and the colonnaded Bath Street by Thomas Baldwin; and in the crescents, such as Camden and Lansdown, the latter by John Palmer who also designed the Pump Room portico. Prior Park (now a Roman Catholic school) by John Wood the Elder was built for Ralph Allen, the new Bath's cofounder, and stands on a hill overlooking the city.

In and about this 'Protestant Venice without the water', setting off the formal architecture and Bath stone, are many parks and gardens—the popular Parade Gardens on the Avon bank, with music in summer; Victoria Park and its botanical gardens, west of Royal Crescent; the garden in Henrietta Park, with its scented plants labelled in braille; and Sydney Gardens at the end of Pulteney Street with its pavilion museum. To this, the Holbourne Menstrie museum (ceramics, miniatures, silver, paintings), can be added an exceptionally fine costume museum in the Assembly Rooms and, at Claverton Manor, $2\frac{1}{2}$ miles away, the American museum of domestic life and American 'primitives'.

Bath Festival is held in June—until 1968 it was directed by Yehudi

Menuhin, and is now under Sir Michael Tippett. The Pump Room for drinking the waters and the Roman Baths are open daily. No. 1 Royal Crescent, built for Wood's own father-in-law, is now a showplace, restored to the semblance of its Georgian heyday. A sample tour of Bath, to see the many houses associated with famous figures of the past, takes about one hour on foot. For a good general prospect of the city, Beechen Cliff or Ralph Allen's folly 'Sham Castle' (1760) are the viewpoints. The question is, can Bath 'get by with only minimal alterations to its fabric', or would a modern Rip Van Winkle in another twenty years find that the planners' answer to present A4 traffic problems had been major destructive changes? Because of its severely disciplined beauty Bath is extremely vulnerable: new building, out of scale, presents another threat.

Betws-y-coed, Carnarvonshire, a grey-stone village strung out on the trunk road from London to Holyhead, has the features of a favourite Victorian honeymoon resort—wooded hills, tumbling waterfalls, crags and spoil heaps rich in flowers, romantic associations—'the oratory in the forest', a humble, unspoilt old church and a new, handsomely furnished mid-Victorian one (Paley and Austin, 1873). The many hotels and villas are evidence of its popularity, maintained in spite of the curse of A5 traffic. The old church has a simple thirteenth-century font and the effigy of a knight in armour who fought for Richard III. The woods are part of the ancient Gwyder Forest centred on Gwyder Castle, with its nearby seventeenth-century chapel with a remarkable cherub-painted ceiling. Picturesque walks through oaks and beeches up to the region of pines, spruces and glacier-smoothed rocks and small lakes are an attraction, second only to visits to the waterfalls—the white Swallow Falls, the brown Conway Falls, the fine falls on the Machno River—and to the ravine of Fairy Glen among scenes celebrated in paint by David Cox. A little further afield lie Llyn Geirionydd and Llyn Crafnant, whose botanically rich crags are in the Cwm Glas National Nature Reserve. To the industrial archaeologist, not only the old lead-mine workings will add to Betws' interest, but the various bridges over the Llugwy, the Lledr and the Conway rivers. Waterloo Bridge (1815), Telford's beautifully built and decorated cast-iron

IRSB—K

structure, is probably the pick of them; but the rugged stone-built Pont-y-pair (fifteenth century) and Pont-ar-Lledr (seventeenth century), the wooden miners' bridge and the castellated railway bridge, two miles up the Lledr valley, have more than mere contrast to offer. Otherwise golf, fishing and climbing are the diversions.

Brecon or **Aberhonddu,** Breconshire, like its Monmouthshire neighbour on the Usk, ABERGAVENNY, provides a good centre for the hills and mountains and lovely side valleys of South Wales, clear of the industrial belt. English-speaking Brecon, whose charter as a borough dates from 1270, has the relics of a castle and town walls, has remained aloof from industry and, in its centre, from modernisation; the former fashionable town houses can still be recognised under their guise as shop or office. Captain's Walk, along a section of the wall between Shire Hall and river, is where French officers, prisoners in the Napoleonic Wars, took exercise. (Brecon is a garrison town and has a military museum.) In addition to the castle, now disarticulated by a hotel and road, there are several old buildings: the chapel of Christ College Public School, once part of a Dominican friary; the massively cruciform church of St John, formerly belonging to a Benedictine priory, now cathedral of the diocese of Swansea and Brecon, and the tithe barn of the priory; the seven-arched bridge over the Usk, originally built in 1563. The town museum provides an historic panorama; for a panorama of the countryside one climbs nearby Pen-y-crug (crowned by an iron-age fort) and can then see the whole circle of mountains—the Black Mountains, the Brecons, Fforest Fawr and Mynydd Eppynt, of which Brecon is the centre. Of the many side valleys, with their old bridges, stone circles and Roman remains, those on the way to Builth (via Upper Chapel), to Battle and to Llandovery are perhaps most worth discovering.

Abergavenny's landmark is the unmistakable Sugar Loaf (1,955ft): Great Skirrid, the other side of the A465, lower but more rugged, was one of the holy mountains climbed by pilgrims (as is Croagh Patrick, Co. Mayo). This busy market town has been a communications centre since Roman times and also had its medieval castle and town walls. Its main street has buildings from the Tudor period onward, but most of its history is concentrated in the museum, next to the castle ruins, and in the parish church, St Mary's, formerly also part of a Benedictine priory, which is especially rich in tombs and effigies and early wood-carving: twenty-four fourteenth-century carved choir stalls have survived.

The whole area is rich in gentlemen's seats, from the late Tudor Llanvihangel Court (open in summer) in the north to Llanover House to the south, home of a former champion of Welsh language and traditions. Abergavenny is the natural gateway to Brecon Beacons National Park, but to climb Blorenge (1,834ft), third of the trio of surrounding hills, from a point just across the Becon–Newport canal, is to realise how close also to industry it lies: from the moorland summit a massive mine tip appears barely half a mile away, whilst not far beyond there is the smoke of Pontypool and of Newport, next to the Severn.

Bridge of Allan, Stirlingshire, for long the favourite inland watering place of Scotland, is an example of a sequestered hamlet rapidly trans-muted into an elegant resort by reason of its neighbouring mineral springs. It grew originally round an ancient Change House (or inn) at the east side of the old bridge, a key position on the main way north. In 1827 it was described as 'a confusion of straw-rooft cottages and massy trees, possessed of a bridge and a mill, together with kailyards, beeskeps, colleys, callants and old inns'. Ten years later the first house of the modern village was erected; by 1845 it had become a flourishing place of about 200 inhabitants and in less than another ten years was known as a spa, with handsome commodious houses and villas 'uniting the rural character of Harrowgate with the town convenience and elegance of Cheltenham'. At any rate there was a library, a reading hall, a billiard room, a curling pond (for winter visitors), a gallery of casts and paintings, three commodious inns, water and gas in the houses and lighting in the streets. By 1856 a Black's guide to the Bridge of Allan and environs had reached its sixth edition.

The cause of all this was the re-opening of a disused copper-mine on the Airthrey estate in 1820, which had led to the discovery of mineral springs. The proprietor of Airthrey, influenced by the success of such waters elsewhere, had their properties analysed, then constructed a well-house and arches over the roof of the mine to safeguard cistern and pipes, providing a flow of about 1,000 gallons a day—sufficient for very large numbers of visitors. Expert opinion declared the saline waters inferior only to those of Cheltenham and Leamington, the strongest purgative waters of England. Later a hydropathic establishment was built with an elegant suite of baths and a daily consultant who had studied at Smedley's, Matlock, and early this century the original Pump Room and Bath House were both re-equipped.

Bridge of Allan has other virtues to recommend it as a resort—an equable climate, 'like Montpellier', protection by the Ochils from north and north-easterly winds, low humidity and grand scenery. Whilst no longer pretending to be either a Cheltenham or a Harrogate —its population, after rising to 1,800 by 1861, has scarcely doubled since then—it is a clean, orderly little town of good stone buildings and tree-lined streets, neither sprawling nor infected by 'towniness'. The bridge is new, but there is still an old mill by the banks of Allan Water and the spa buildings still function as part of one of the hotels; a golf course, tennis courts and bowling greens, and the Strathallan games (first Saturday in August) are later attractions. The river Allan is open for fishing (best for trout in April to June, for salmon in July to September); but above all, the place offers those charms which a regular visitor, R. L. Stevenson, summed up as 'the grass and the fir trees and the river, the sheep and the sunshine and the shadows of the fir trees', in proximity to such scenery as that of the Trossachs, Loch Lomond, the Braes of Balquhidder and the Ochil country as far as Gleneagles. A hundred or more years ago visitors to Bridge of Allan used to admire the 'stupendous' iron works at Carron, near Falkirk (as did Silas Neville in 1775): in future they may come to see Bridge of Allan itself as a new university town.

Bridge of Earn, Perthshire, has the oldest natural medicinal waters in Scotland, with five mineral wells at Pitkeathly, a mile away. A sizeable village, at a point where the main routes to Perth cross the river, it makes a pleasant resort with charming views, hotels and access to much attractive scenery.

Buxton's elegant town centre, laid out by the fifth Duke of Devonshire in the eighteenth century, is an admirable foil to the surrounding wooded dales and majestic moorland of the Derbyshire Peak National Park. It cannot be expected that the whole town's development is in accord with the splendid Crescent (1780), the Great Stables and the Pavilion Gardens (opened by the then Duke of Devonshire in 1871). Whilst the architectural heritage of the central area is protected by the Civic Amenities Act (1967) as a conservation area, supermarkets and national multiples are well represented among the shops—an acceptance of the trend that has helped to save a town in a somewhat tucked-away Pennine position from becoming a museum-piece. Buxton welcomes its shoppers with free and plentiful parking facilities (especially appreciated by bargain hunters on open-air market Saturdays) and has plans to create a completely traffic-free shopping street adjacent to the Quadrant and Crescent. Over a dozen hotels and restaurants, from the palatial and fashion-conscious to the 'homely with good food', meet both conference and casual visitors' needs. It is hoped to revive Buxton's Music Festival.

When one has viewed the Crescent (architect, John Carr of York) and St Ann's Well, the Pump Room (housing the Information Bureau), the former opera house (now a cinema), admired the remarkable unsupported dome of the Devon Royal Hospital (the former Great Stables) and period features in the Pavilion Gardens, the oldest public building that remains is St Ann's Church (seventeenth-century), descendant of the Well Chapel, which stood on the site of the present town hall. For those interested in the associations and relics of a town with a long history as a resort or in the important pre-historic finds made in the neighbourhood, the museum is an obvious information centre. For others the neighbourhood itself will be the chief attraction —the Goyt Valley and Peak Cavern (Castleton) near at hand, Haddon Hall and Chatsworth House within easy motoring range (via Bakewell). The Derbyshire dales can be left to speak for themselves.

Cheltenham Spa, Gloucestershire, is the present writer's choice for an English inland resort comparable in elegance and atmosphere with those of Europe. It is right in scale, in situation, in climate, in liveliness and 'perhaps the most beautiful thoroughfare in the country' articulates it. By 1860 it was deemed to possess 'more resources for occupation and amusement than any other provincial town' and to be one of the most eligible for residence.

This Regency town, covering eight tree-shaded square miles on a sheltered ridge between the Cotswolds and the Vale of Severn, developed from a large village with mineral springs (discovered in 1715) and a primitive Pump Room into a spa, after the visit of George III (fully recorded by Fanny Burney), and the rapid growth of its reputation for curing liverish colonial administrators, following the Duke of Wellington's recommendation. Plans for an entirely new town, carried out between 1800 and 1840, resulted in a much higher proportion of buildings more completely in harmony with each other and more integrated with their surroundings than in most other resorts. Chief architects were J. B. Papworth—Lansdown Place, Montpellier Parade and the Rotunda (1826, now neglected); J. B. Forbes—the Pittville Pump Room, for the only natural alkaline water in Britain, (built in 1825 and restored after World War II); R. W. and C. Jearrad the Queen's Hotel, terminal to the Promenade (completed in 1838 and 1825 respectively); and G. A. Underwood—the Masonic Hall, the church in Portland Street and various terraces and Greek villas. Many houses still have their delicate Regency ironwork verandahs and balconies: Montpellier Walk has its shops separated by caryatids, a veritable street of statues. With the great chestnut trees and flower baskets on the Promenade, the coloured umbrellas and cafe tables and the Imperial Gardens adjacent, with the flowers banked on street corners and the miles of tree-lined avenues, the effect is given of a town within a park or of the two comprising one indivisible entity: one acre indeed in every ten of the town's total is park. It is an effort at times in Cheltenham to recall that one is in England.

Apart from its Ladies' College and College for Boys (whose 'walking-out' areas in the town are kept strictly separate), its classical frontages and other reminders of civilised values, Cheltenham has kept pace with the best in modern living. Its music festival is one of the most important in the country, its fashion houses stem from Bond Street and Paris; the élite of its hotels and restaurants combine Regency style and up-to-date cuisine and comfort. Whatever one may feel about the development of jet aircraft (first successfully produced in a Cheltenham workshop), the availability of a first-class airport within five miles is another undoubted asset to a town already the junction of express road services to all parts. And, of course, the treasury of Cotswold villages lies only just over the doorstep.

Crieff, the popular Perthshire health resort—originally the Burgh of Regality of Drummond—has claims to be the most picturesquely situated hill-town in Scotland. Close to the river Earn, on the wooded southern slopes of the Knock, offshoot of the Grampian range, it stands sentinel at one of the gateways (the Sma' Glen) to the Perthshire Highlands and at the same time commands wide views towards the Lowlands. (A line drawn more or less directly from near Glasgow to Aberdeen would divide the Highlands from the rest of Scotland: a hundred and fifty years ago it was considered to mark the border between 'civilised' and 'savage'; today the wildness of the scenery north of the line, not of the way of life of its inhabitants, makes the difference.)

Crieff has, in addition to the lovely scenery of upper Strathearn, the equable climate, pine-smelling air and sparkling water to recommend it for health and also considerable historical interest. It was a 'considerable town for these parts' in 1775 (Silas Neville). The octagonal mercat cross of the burgh stands in High Street, a relic associated with Rob Roy; there are ancient stocks and across the road the red sandstone runic Cross of Crieff, probably of twelfth-century origin. In the town hall (the old Tolbooth, built 1665), the timber of the 'kind gallows' can be seen, a relic of the times when the King's Steward of Strathearn exercised both high, low and middle justice. Prince Charles Edward spent a night, in 1745, at an inn in Crieff—now replaced by the National Commercial Bank. Only the square tower remains of Drummond Castle, two miles to the south—partly demolished in 1745 to prevent its occupation by Hanoverian troops—but it has a fine collection of old armour, fine gardens and a 'romantic situation' (Neville), with a prospect extending as far as Dundee. The remains of Ferntower House, on the south-east slope of the Knock, recall Sir David, hero of Seringapatam, who died there in 1829. Of perhaps more significance, at any rate to Scotsmen, is the library at Innerpeffray, three miles away, founded by David Drummond, Baron Madertie (d. 1692)—the first free library in Scotland and full of irreplaceable treasures.

It goes almost without saying that Crieff has fine parks, six in all, sylvan walks, a nature trail, a superb golf course, fishing, yachting and water ski-ing (on Loch Earn), and abundant choice of accommodation in Hydro (200 bedrooms) or unpretentious boarding houses. A well-known writer has chosen this as the best place in Scotland to grow up and grow old in—as did the several noblemen whose seats grace the locality.

Dolgelley, county town of Merionethshire, looks up to Cader Idris as Coniston, in the Lake District, looks up to the Old Man (Ald Maen = stony hill) and gains as much from the association. The Georgian shire hall and the little square, into which narrow streets lead from many directions, are otherwise almost all that dignifies a capital, than which only five in Great Britain are smaller—Cromarty, Inverary, Dornoch, Dingwall and Beaumaris. (Blaenau Ffestiniog is Merioneth's *largest* town.) An old Parliament House was pulled down in 1882 (to be rebuilt in a private park at Newtown) and nearly all ancient buildings have gone, but metropolitan names abound in the streets and little squares—Smithfield, Eldon, Lombard, Baker, Skinner, Waterloo, etc. The town owes its popularity as a tourist resort almost entirely to its surroundings, for which it is almost unrivalled in Wales. It effectively combines the characteristic features, river, rock and wood, and mountain scenery, of Llangollen, Betws-y-coed and Beddgelert, in its own valley of the Wnion, its rocks of Mynydd-y-Gader and the heights of Mynydd Moel (eastern peak of Cader Idris). It offers good fishing, good hunting—for ferns rather than foxes—and abundance of good walks. Apart from the scenic beauty of the walk from Dolgelley to Barmouth—ranked by Ruskin as second only to that of the walk from Barmouth to Dolgelley—there are the well-known Torrent Walk, the Precipice Walk and walks in the Aran Glen and Abergwynant Valley, closer to Cader Idris. Of the latter mountain it need only be said that visitors since Charles Darwin's day have found its cirques of cliffs, corrie lakes, great scree slopes and crystalline rock, coupled with the

views along its six-mile ridge, irresistible. Incidentally Dolgelley has
more than one meritorious hotel (with Welsh lamb, local lobster and
salmon in season) in or near, and a golf course, a cinema and an endowed
girls' school.

Droitwich, Worcestershire, still functions as a spa, although closure
of its baths is forecast. Its character, like that of many former spas, is
changing but its attractions remain. As it is the first town to the south-
west beyond the proposed Birmingham green belt and is surrounded
by pleasant countryside, the attractions seem likely to be preserved,
wherever possible, in the current expansion and development scheme.

Old pre-spa Droitwich has some good architectural features: six-
teenth-, seventeenth- and eighteenth-century houses in Friar Street and
High Street; typical Worcestershire black-and-white half-timbered
houses in St Andrew's Street; an inn with an ecclesiastical window
(the Old Cock); and the old Elizabethan Manor of Wyche, now frontispiece of the Raven Hotel. This last with the Worcestershire Hotel and
St Andrew's Brine Baths on two of its other sides help to make
Victoria Square an appropriate town centre. St Andrew's church has
thirteenth-century features and St Peter's, south of the town, some
early fourteenth-century stained glass and a Norman chancel, but it is
the Church of the Sacred Heart and St Catherine, on the Worcester
road, which compels notice. A series of modern mosaics cover most of
the walls and roof, depicting biblical scenes and the life of the Droitwich saint, Richard (de Burford), born *c* 1197, later Richard de la
Wyche, Bishop of Chichester under Henry III. The mosaics are in the
manner of Ravenna.

Apart from pleasant parks and an open air 'sea-bathing' lido, excep-
tional hotel and golf facilities, Droitwich offers considerable neighbourhood interest. Near at hand is the village of Salwarpe, with its
sixteenth-century half-timbered Court, family seat of the Talbots,
its Georgian rectory and an old mill house near the canal. Further
afield, but not too far, are the Malvern Hills, the Cotswolds, the
Severn Valley and Stratford-on-Avon (20 miles). Besides the Shakespeare season there (April to November), the Three Choirs Festival,
held in the cathedrals at Hereford, Gloucester and Worcester (1972), in

rotating years, during the first week of September, can conveniently be enjoyed from Droitwich as the centre.

Dulverton, Somerset, on a renowned fishing river, the Barle, and in the middle of the red-deer hunting country, has been south-east Exmoor's shopping headquarters probably for the last six hundred years. Its pure water, bracing air and perfect drainage have since re-commended it to those with a taste for healthy exercise amid picturesque scenery and comparative solitude. The town nestles at the foot of steep hills in an amphitheatric expansion of the Barle valley, where the river emerges from the ravine through which it descends from Exmoor. Though a little dull and jumbled architecturally, it fits well into its singularly beautiful site. There is character in buildings and inhabitants and hotels—one of which was formerly the old rectory—and an absence of haste about everything except the river. The tower of the church (rebuilt in 1855) is thirteenth century and the sycamore tree which almost hides it is not less than 250 years old.

The principal objective of sightseers is the prehistoric clapper bridge known as Tarr (Tor) Steps, about five miles up-river near Hawkridge. Of massive character, this oldest bridge in Britain comprises 19 openings, 16 'wet' and 3 'dry'; the piers are formed of flags laid horizontally and long slabs extend from pier to pier, making the crossing about 50 paces. It is held together by the weight of stone. Tor, pronounced Tar(r), has supposed associations with Thor and traditionally the devil was the architect of this cyclopean structure—composed actually of the cheapest and most easily procured materials of the district.

Other sights, nearer town, are Pixton Park prominently placed at the top of a steep ascent, once home of the eighteenth-century owner of Exmoor's first pack of staghounds; Barlinch Priory ruins on the Dunster road; and the view from Hele bridge on the Exe, where the river flows through a narrow valley enclosed by wooded hills. The fair at Bampton, $4\frac{1}{2}$ miles to the south-east, is famous for the sale, in late October, of rounded-up Exmoor ponies. Sportsmen, of course, are well provided for with hunting, hacking, salmon and trout fishing and rough shooting on the wide expanses of moor and woodland.

Dunblane, Perthshire, two miles north of Bridge of Allan, was an early Victorian spa, with an historic cathedral, a fifteenth-century single arch bridge over Allan Water and a mill also claiming to be that celebrated in the song. The passion for building hydropathics struck Scotland forcibly in the mid-Victorian era; most of them are now put to other purposes, but Dunblane's retains its position as central Scotland's leading hotel.

The settlement was founded by the Celtic Missionary, St Blane, in the seventh century and made the seat of a bishopric by David I. Its cathedral, dedicated to St Blane, is thirteenth century, and dominates the burgh; for three hundred years its nave, which collapsed at the end of the sixteenth century, remained roofless; restoration came in 1893, and in 1914 to the choir, which had meantime served as the only place of worship. The woodwork of the choir has some of Scotland's finest carving, and there are six fifteenth-century stalls. The churchyard is noted for its quaint tombstones and epitaphs. The row of traditional 'little houses' in Kirk Street and Sinclair Street, near the cathedral, now serve as a retreat and a church conference centre. Queen Victoria School, an impressive building in the Scottish tradition, opened in 1908 as a national memorial to the Queen and to Scottish soldiers and sailors who fell in the South African War, affords free board and education to the sons of Scottish servicemen and was extended in 1963.

Dunblane's attractions as a touring base are the same as those of Bridge of Allan: it has also 'enticing walks' near at hand. Bishop's Walk by the river (named after Bishop Leighton, seventeenth-century donor of the Diocesan Library in the Cross), a walk through the Haugh and the Haining by the ruins of the Bishop's Palace, through the glen of Allan Water towards Bridge of Allan, by the old Doune Road to Anchor-cross Hill or by Newton Loan and the hydro to Sheriffmuir woods for magnificent mountain views, including Ben Lomond—these are but a few of the alternatives. The Gathering Stone, behind the woods, another notable viewpoint, was visited by the Duke of Argyll, on reconnaissance, before the indecisive battle with forces of the Old Pretender on Sheriffmuir in November 1715.

Epping's forest is the remains of the greater forest of Waltham which once reached to the town of that name, where Henry VIII stayed for hunting, and almost to the walls of London. It extends now from Epping town for about ten miles, up to halfway being over a mile in width, then narrowing and becoming less continuous towards Wanstead and Leyton, as London encroaches on each side. With its thick beech and hornbeam coverts, its grassy glades and rougher clearings—best enjoyed in autumn and winter solitude—it remains a fine recreation ground even by European standards. Had not enclosure of forest land been halted in 1874, and a decree been passed to recover all illegal enclosures made between 1851 and 1871, the forest would be only about half its present size (*c* 6,000 acres). When Queen Victoria dedicated it to public use for all time, planting a commemoratory tree on High Beech Hill, in May 1882, all London's East End rejoiced. The Epping Staghunt, however, a survival of the privilege granted to London citizens by Edward IV of hunting in Waltham Forest, had already been brought to an end, in 1853, by the enclosures. Today deer run wild and unmolested, safeguarded in this natural animal sanctuary. High Beech—whose popularity in later Edwardian days has left the overgrown remains of wrought-iron tea-houses—and Connaught Water, both on the western side, are favourite Forest resorts: as are the Tudor-style Royal Forest Hotel, near Chingford, and the Queen Elizabeth Hunting Lodge, with its museum. This southern end of the Forest, with its lake and bathing pond, becomes less distinguishable from other London commons. Alternative points from which to explore are Buckhurst Hill and Theydon Bois; the village of Upshire with its painted weatherboarded terraces should be seen—while there is time.

Epping town, on a northerly ridge, has a long, wide main street, as befits an old coaching town, and a weekly market (Monday): formerly its butter and cheese were highly regarded. The present parish church, St John, is Victorian; the former one, at Epping Upland, two miles away, medieval, with a sixteenth-century brick tower. Those who stay at the Bell (Motor) Hotel may care to recall that Pepys enjoyed a night's 'stopover' there in 1660.

Grasmere, Westmorland, Mecca of the Lake District for admirers of the Wordsworths, no longer enjoys the seclusion which attracted the poet to it: now it is very much the tourist centre instead of 'this little unsuspected paradise'. Barns and cottages are given over to hand-weaving, pottery, local painting, Victoriana, National Trust information and souvenirs of all sorts; a large car-park, tea-shops and half a dozen hotels, of various degrees of sophistication, anticipate the tourist's needs. One hotel was commended by Wordsworth himself and his name brings queues still, in summer, to Dove Cottage, just off the A591, the poet's and his sister's first residence when they settled in Grasmere in December 1799 (it became later the home of De Quincey); to the Wordsworth museum, which faces the cottage: in spring, especially, to Rydal Mount, the poet's later home, to Rydal Church, whose site he helped to choose, and Rash Field or 'Dora's Field' whose daffodils he planted for his daughter. All are at an easy distance from Grasmere. And, of course, all seek Grasmere church, unadorned externally, but containing the Wordsworth memorial tablet and, in a corner of the churchyard, under a yew, the plain tombstones to the poet and his family.

Grasmere has its 'rush-bearing' in August, a custom preserved from times when the church aisles were not covered with matting and the pews with carpet, but when rushes were used to keep feet off the cold floor. A gathering of rushes was made each summer and they were carried with ceremony to the church; nowadays garlands and rushes, trimmed, are borne on frames by children in procession and placed in the church, and a short festival service is held, with a hymn specially written by a friend of Wordsworth. Grasmere sports, also held in August, include Cumberland wrestling, the 'Guide's Race' up and down steep fells, and hound trails. From Rydal, about mid-August, one can watch sheep dog trials and so complete the round of traditional sports. Sometimes also one can see a turn-out of gigs, governess carts, traps and four-in-hands got up in old style, including drivers and passengers. At the end of the season, in late October, there is an Antiques Fair.

Harrogate, Yorkshire, town of stately hotels and handsome terraces, of large open greens and beautifully-kept gardens, of sunblinds and shaded walks, maintains a stylish, prosperous look in the West Riding tradition. The Royal Pump Room (1842) with its small Victorian museum, the Royal Baths, the Kursaal (now Royal Hall), the Old Swan Hotel (1820), the White Hart (1848), now a hospital, and the Crown (1847) opposite, give to the old spa centre a sense of permanence and distinction. Flower-beds are everywhere, with sun terraces and pavilions and an open-air bandstand in the adjacent Valley Gardens. The shops include up-to-the-minute fashion displays, select old-fashioned grocers and an unusual range of antique dealers. Disc parking encourages the motorist to make Harrogate both his pleasure and his shopping centre; there is also a diesel shuttle service to Leeds.

Something is always going on in Harrogate, at the repertory theatre, in the concert halls, at the exhibition centre, in the field of festivals and sporting events. The spring Flower Show, held in April, almost rivals that of Chelsea. The Hallé Festival of Music and the Great Yorkshire Show in July, the Festival of Arts and Sciences in August and the Antiques Fair in September exert far more than local appeal. Between-times conferences and trade fairs, car rallies and special flower and live-stock shows crowd upon each other. A resident expressed his relish at the friendly bustle and matter-of-factness of the town on returning from an equally stylish south-coast resort: 'a little too tidy, refined and clean, having an almost sterilised appearance'. A sign of the community spirit is the rebirth of the Grand Opera House as the Harrogate Theatre, achieved by local effort.

Beyond the Stray or Two Hundred Acre, with the pump rooms of Tewit Well and St John's Well, beyond Harlow Moor and the horti-cultural trial gardens there are other attractions within a few miles: Knaresborough, with its castle commanding the gorge of the Nidd and its petrifying well, Brimham Rocks near Pateley Bridge, Fountains Abbey, Rudding Park and Newby Hall with their treasures of porcelain, pictures and Gobelin tapestries, Bramham Park with its Versailles-style gardens. For centre *and* setting there is no other place like Harrogate in northern England.

Ilkley, Yorkshire, has a fine situation, with wild moors, natural woodland, a pastoral riverside and the delights of upper Wharfedale beyond. A walk on the west of the town up Heber's Ghyll to the 2,000-year-old Swastika Stone will reveal their presence and promise. The town centre itself, of four streets forming roughly a square, lacks distinction, although the wide and breezy Grove is attractive in summer greenery. Here the parish church and manor house (museum) in Church Street are the buildings of interest: the latter has its Elizabethan stone mullion windows, open fireplaces and carved beams. The church, much restored, has a fine early-English entrance and a western tower of the Decorated period, and, in the churchyard, three ancient stone crosses (recorded by Camden) belonging to the transition period from Anglican to Viking and therefore especially noteworthy. The modern church, St Margaret's, up the hillside, is the work of Norman Shaw.

Ilkley's ex-hydros also lie uphill, standing sentinel over the valley spread of the residential town and having the same solid dark stone appearance as the former grammar school, opened in 1893. Solid Victorian boarding houses are in evidence here too, along Wells Road, Crossbeck Road and Cowpasture Road—often converted to flats. A little higher there is Ilkley Tarn, popular for summer promenading and winter skating; higher still on the moorland slope White Wells (and baths) stands out as a conspicuous landmark. From there Rocky Valley and the well-known Cow and Calf Rocks are within strolling distance. Both on these moors and in Middleton Woods on the other side of the valley there are nature trails. Easy access to places of such varied interest as Beamsley Beacon, Bolton Abbey, Harewood House and Haworth (for *Wuthering Heights*)—the latter by direct hourly bus service—adds to the enviability of Ilkley's situation. To cater for the summer flow of visitors there are plenty of cafes, restaurants, apartments and hotels of character and comfort. The Wharfedale Musical Festival takes place there in May. In July, when public schools are 'down' and the Grove a sunny morning-rendezvous for their products and their parents, Ilkley recovers a faintly fashionable air.

Inverleithen, Peeblesshire, an early nineteenth-century watering place, had mineral springs named and claimed as the prototype of St Ronan's

Well (Scott). The spring on the slope of Lee Pen Hill, called Dow's Well prior to 1823, supplied waters similar to those of Harrogate and encouraged Lord Traquair to provide a pump house, reading rooms and a verandah, reconstructed in 1896. Nowadays St Ronan's works supply quality aerated waters. Before its waters brought the 'attractive little grey stone town' into favour as a resort, industry had already given it some repute. Caerlee Mill, built in 1790, is probably the oldest mill in use on the Borders; the manufacture of Tweed cloth and hosiery continues. Traquair House (whose gates were locked after the visit of Prince Charles Edward in 1745 and have never since been opened) is said to be the oldest in Scotland, with a tower reputed to go back a thousand years. The first recorded royal visitor was Alexander I in 1107. No alterations have been made to the structure for over three hundred years, and most of the furnishings have remained unaltered for over one hundred and fifty. Carved bears on either side of the main gateway suggest more links with Scott—Tully-Veolen and the Bears of Bradwardine (*Waverley*).

Associations apart, Inverleithen, if not distinguished architecturally, is nicely set among smooth round-headed hills, close to the junction of the Leithen and the Tweed and by any road out of town one is led into some of the finest Lowland scenery. Yarrow Water and St Mary's Loch are both within easy reach; the Scott country, Abbotsford and the Borderland are not far away, it is a good walking centre, has its Border Games (in July) and in the 'Cleikum Week' (August) the ceremony of 'Cleiking the De'il'—a reminder of St Ronan's battle with that adversary when he came to the valley in 737 AD.

Keswick, Cumberland, a busy market town, is the natural base for exploring that part of central and northern Lakeland which is less accessible from Windermere or Ambleside. The profile of Skiddaw at the ends of roads, the proximity of Derwentwater and the perfection of Borrowdale tempt the visitor afield. Once a centre for mining prospectors (gold, silver, copper were found nearby), subsequently for the manufacture of linsey-woolsey stuffs, edge tools and black lead pencils, Keswick has character.

Round the focal building of the town, a somewhat foreign-looking black and white Moothall (1813), spreads an open street market (Saturday). Climbing equipment shops and quick service cafes, fashion boutiques and photographers elbow each other in the narrow thorough-fares and alleyways: displays of antiques, of pictures and prints and antiquarian books, lurk in unexpected corners. High and Low Fitz Parks, on the north bank of the Greta, close to the town centre, have both games facilities and a museum with many original manuscripts of Lakes writers. Only a short walk away, by St John's churchyard, lies Derwentwater with its boat-landings and Ruskin monument on the promontory of Friar's Crag, from which point nearly the whole lake is visible. After prolonged downpours the Falls of Lodore, three miles off at the other end of the lake, can actually be heard from here.

Within the town there is a wide range of hotel and boarding house accommodation, from the largest hotel in Lakeland to small terraced houses in localities like Skiddaw Street: other luxury hotel and cottage hospitality can be found up and down Borrowdale and in hamlets on the approaches to Bassenthwaite lake. (During the annual summer convention casual accommodation is hard to come by.) The parish church, St Kentigern's, at Crosthwaite about a mile from the town centre, has a fine monument of Southey, with an inscription by Words-worth, and in the churchyard Southey's grave; its vicar, for a quarter of century, was Canon Rawnsley, founder of the National Trust. Greta Hall, on a low hill north of the town, was Southey's residence for forty years, in succession to Coleridge, and was a gathering ground of the poets and their friends. Somewhat further out there is the bronze age Castlerigg Stone Circle, almost a hundred feet in diameter: the visitor here finds himself in the centre of an immense circle of mountains, Saddleback, Skiddaw, Helvellyn, the Scafells, etc., with a panoramic view nearly one hundred miles in circumference. Castle Head, the best viewpoint close to Keswick, is all that is left of a volcano belonging to the formative period of Lakeland geology.

Keswick has to offer the grandest scene of its kind in the kingdom, worth remembering when the press of rucksacks and ropes, the clump of boots, the exhausts of motor-cars and the eddying crowds of tourists make its streets barely tolerable.

Leamington Spa, Warwickshire, indulges its residents and visitors in 'Spamenities', to the tune of some fifty 'live entertainments' in an average summer month. Between June and October it casts its net of public attractions wide with a competitive festival of music, dancing and drama, an open bowls tournament, a water-safety gala, an international archery tournament, an open art exhibition, a folk dance festival and a dozen silver and brass band concerts. It maintains the triple reputation of a stylish Midlands' shopping centre, a busy conference town and an important physical medicine centre. With all this Leamington manages still to evoke the atmosphere of a gracious and leisurely inland resort. How is it achieved? By space, brightness, cleanliness in its streets and squares and tree-lined Parade, its public grounds and gardens, and by abundant car-parking facilities. One is first tempted to come and then to take it slowly in order to take it all in.

The general plan of Leamington, north of the river Leam, owed a great deal to the influence of Dr Henry Jephson, and its 'Royal' prefix dates from his reception there, in 1838, of the young Queen Victoria, though the Pump Room (rebuilt in 1925) dates from 1814. The fine Regency and early Victorian terraced houses have formed the town's chief glory ever since: Lansdowne Crescent, Clarendon Square, Newbold Terrace and the sweep of the Lower Parade can compare not unfavourably with Bath. The intermingling of the Jephson Gardens, the Pump Room gardens, of tree-lined avenues like Holly Walk, Northumberland Terrace, Hamilton Terrace and Regent Grove adds an almost continental air. Some streets behind the Parade tend towards the run-down, but the total effect is elegant. The Art Gallery, adjoining the Public Library, appropriately displays bygones relating to Leamington's growth as a town and the Victorian costumes of its heyday as a spa.

For the tourist intent on seeing Shakespeare country or the Cotswolds —Bourton-on-the-Water, Broadway, Chipping Campden, Chipping Norton, Stow-on-the-Wold, etc.—Leamington is well placed and well served by coach. It is also barely half an hour by express train from Birmingham.

Llandrindod Wells, Radnorshire, a little over midway on the A483 from Chester to Swansea, and about midway also from Cardigan Bay to the A49, sits pretty in central Wales for tourists who tire of Aberystwyth—or the journey to it. It is a town of the garden city type, developed from a straggling riverside hamlet as the celebrity of the spa and the coming of the railway encouraged speculative building, much of it during the last eighty years. There are no slums, no pollution, no black spots, no meanness or overcrowding, and the introduction of light industry has been discreet. The Spa Baths and Pump Room and Pavilion in Rock Park provide the showpiece, surrounded by flowers, lawns, woods and water. Just across the railway there are the Grand Pavilion, cinema and recreation ground: then the Temple Gardens and town hall, library and museum also in garden surroundings. Natural rock formations, common and woodland have been used to give the impression that the town is part of the countryside and the countryside is in the town. Several of the large hotels are in their own spacious grounds. The old parish Church of the Trinity, situated on a hill overlooking the lake south-east of the town, gives it its name and is the church from which Welsh bishops elected their first Archbishop.

Bowls, golf and fishing rank high among Llandrindod's sporting attractions. Rock Park's bowling greens are claimed as among the world's finest and attract many clubs on holiday as well as national championship meetings; the Bowls Festival is held in August. The golf course, one of a few, like Church Stretton's, at over 1,000 feet, offers panoramic views, as far as Plynlimon and Brecon Beacons, and resilient mountain turf; the September Open Meeting has reached its jubilee. Fishing for trout, salmon, carp, tench and bream can be enjoyed on preserves of the river Ithon, on the white poplar-fringed lake and in reaches of the upper Wye, as well as in private waters belonging to hotels and in the not distant Birmingham Corporation reservoir. The town has become a centre for many national and international motoring and motor-cycling events, ACU and RAC, and is a checkpoint in the Monte Carlo rally.

While exerting centripetal attraction to its seasonal festivals, drama in May, the Eisteddfod in October, and its many club and conference functions, Llandrindod is a centrifuge for the other attractions of Wales and its borders. Rhayader is almost on the doorstep; Ludlow, Shrewsbury and Hereford are within an easy day's return journey; so also are Cardiff and the resorts of Cardigan Bay. For the many mountain passes and beauty spots—Symonds Yat, Devil's Bridge, Tintern, Llanthony—which demand to be seen, Llandrindod is an ideal starting point. And to it, in turn, come express motor coaches daily from London, the northern and eastern counties, the Midlands and even the south coast.

Llangollen, Denbighshire, once a posting station on the London–Holyhead road, has been popular ever since Welsh tourism began closely followed by the 'romantic' discovery of Wales. Aptly described as 'the picturesque dream in unlawful mood', it has magnificent limestone cliffs, medieval ruins, industrial monuments and intriguing personal associations. The near-vertical forms of the Trefor and Eglwyseg Rocks, between which the Dee flows, offer scarcely less architectural satisfaction than the substantial remains of the Cistercian Abbey of Valle Crucis two miles to the north. Only a caravan site has marred the picture of church and monastery, beautifully placed in the valley by monks from near Welshpool. The cross, with its scarcely visible ninth-century inscription to a Prince of Powys, stands a short way further north, quite near the A542.

The town itself, once famous for its beer and the manufacture of Welsh flannel, centres on Trefor Bridge—of early twelfth-century origin. Apart from the old mills by the river there is also Telford's Llangollen canal to attract the industrial historian. Designed in 1805, as a navigable feeder to the Ellesmere canal, part of the Shropshire Union, it can still be explored by 'long boat' and has fine rock cuttings, and a beautiful weir (Horseshoe Falls). The 19-arch Dee aqueduct, 120 feet above the water, is $3\frac{1}{2}$ miles east of the town. Of more general interest perhaps is Plas Newydd, the unique black-and-white house (open to the public) where the 'Ladies of Llangollen' settled after 'eloping' from the boredom of Kilkenny, in 1780. It is decorated with pieces of wood-carving from all over Europe, brought as presents or tribute to the Lady Eleanor Butler and the Hon Sarah Ponsonby, whose visitors included Scott, Wordsworth, Shelley and Wellington. Their monument on the south wall of the church is lively and amusing: the view from their house of medieval Castell Dinas Bran, on its 900-foot outcrop in the vale, built by the son of the founder of Valle Crucis, notably romantic.

The colourful international Eisteddfod takes place in July in a field upstream of Trefor Bridge, where countries from all over the world send song and dance teams to compete.

Lyndhurst, Hampshire, although close to Southampton, has not yet sacrificed to suburban influences its individuality as capital of the New Forest. A long street rising from east to west, crowned at its highest point by the impressive Church of St Michael and two large hotels, one at the eastern end, the other at the top of High Street, form the main structure of the town, which is comparable in simplicity to Woodhall Spa and has domestic building and population of similar order. Its situation, however, makes it a much busier tourist centre. Just as the administrators of the Forest Courts, or courts of Swainmote, foregather here, at Verderers' Hall in High Street (to be a verderer one must own at least 75 acres with common rights), so everyone comes to Lyndhurst who visits the New Forest. Now reduced to an area about the same size as the Isle of Wight, its afforestation was due to the order of William the Conqueror; Charles II and William III both ordered more planting; now under Crown right about one sixth of the whole area is enclosed and planted. The rest comprises a varied countryside, rich in wild life, in old earthworks and barrows and in delightful villages. Before exploring them most people seek out Rufus Stone, in a glade at Stony Cross, near Castle Markwood: it marks the site of the oak tree which diverted the flight of the arrow, shot by Sir Walter Tyrell at a hart and fatal to King Rufus, out hunting deer on 2 August 1100. Sir Walter fled to Normandy and thereafter was regarded as a regicide: the king's body was discovered by a charcoal burner and taken in his cart to Winchester for burial. The memorial stone was erected by Earl de la Warr in 1745: the tree itself has long perished. Markwood Keep, itself now barely traceable, was a royal hunting castle under the Conqueror.

Beaulieu, both for its own sake as an unspoilt village, and for its beautiful Cistercian Abbey remains, and its Montague Motor Museum (containing also bicycles, motor cycles and aircraft), is perhaps the greatest nearby rival attraction to Lyndhurst; but Brockenhurst should be visited: it has excellent shops and hotels, handmade 'New Forest toys' and Morant Hall where the New Forest Hunt Ball and other Forest functions are held: the place, in fact, to feel its social and sporting pulse.

Malvern, Worcestershire, 'The Arts Centre of the West', as it is called by the Theatre Trust, and its motto 'Levavi oculos meos in montes' taken together fairly sum up this old resort's appeal and character. Few former spas could match the beauty of its situation and surroundings, at the foot of a nine-mile range of open hills, with views from their summits extending up to fifty miles. Since the first productions of George Bernard Shaw's plays its Theatrical Festival has been extended to provide a wide variety of first-class entertainment and is supported by the additional attractions of a modern cinema and large Winter Gardens and an open-air heated swimming pool. The fact that 'Malvern water', says Dr John Wall, 'is famed for containing just nothing at all', just as it certainly did not detract from Malvern's esteem in 'cure' days, so it does not impair its bottled sales today—over a million annually. The Queen takes it on her journeys abroad.

Early relics of the spa can be seen in a cottage above Great Malvern, built 1815 for visitors to St Ann's Well, and in Wells House School, the original well-house, accommodation for the Holy Well. Lloyds Bank now stands where Dr Wilson set up business in Belle Vue Terrace. The 'Bridge of Sighs', which connected the former Tudor House and Holyrood House, built by Dr Gully, co-founder of the water cure, for men and women, is now part of the Tudor Hotel, while Townsend House, built by Dr Grindrod, is now the Music School of Malvern College. The college itself was formerly a railway hotel equipped with all types of baths: another 'cure' establishment, Priessnitz House, has become Park View Hotel. The two white houses below the boating lake in Priory Park, fed by the chalybeate spring, were formerly bath cottage and pump room.

The Priory church, in the centre of Malvern, a blend of the Norman and Perpendicular, dates from 1085: it was saved from destruction in the Dissolution by payment of a heavy fine. Its medieval glass, its hand-made fifteenth-century tiles, its dark oak monastic choir stalls with their carved misericords are especially noteworthy. Little Malvern Priory, founded in 1171, although mostly ruined, is also used for services. The nearby Little Malvern Court, of thirteenth-century origin, once housed Catherine of Aragon and still has one of her trunks and a quilt.

With its many schools and colleges, its dignified hotels and terraced lay-out, Malvern shares in the atmosphere common to Bath, Buxton and Cheltenham, even though it is now more of a dormitory town for Worcester and Birmingham. At Three Counties Show time (second week in June) and during the Festival Theatre season it is both gay and crowded: for those who prefer quietude there are always the hills, with plentiful conservators' car-parks and picnic areas to disperse the crowd. From the highest point, Worcestershire Beacon, a toposcope enables one to identify hills and towns spread over about one sixth of the whole land-surface of England and Wales. (The best chance of obtaining this extensive panorama is after rain in May or June.) The characteristic appearance of the Malverns, seemingly heightened in a dry summer, is consonant with the name's derivation from Moel-Bryn, meaning Bare Hill, and with the range's volcanic rock formation, probably the oldest in Europe.

The **Matlocks,** Derbyshire, forming with Bakewell and Buxton the axis of the Peak National Park, and all on the A6, comprise by reason of their setting one of the most spectacular of English resorts. The whole area, included under Matlock UDC, from Little Rowsley in the north to Cromford in the south, has rock and river scenery of a high order. From the vantage point of Clack Rocks (reached from Cromford) the Matlocks themselves are almost hidden in the deep valley of the Derwent. Gone are the hydropathic and other remedial treatments for which Matlock formerly stood in such high esteem, but their physical reminders are there in Smedley's Memorial Hospital, and in the County Council Offices (Smedley's Hydro) at Matlock Bank, in the College of Education housed in two other former large hydros, in the Grand

Pavilion (Pump Room), the terraces and slippery woodland paths and the Aquarium (Fountain Baths) at Matlock Bath. The Victoria Prospect Tower and Heights of Abraham are open throughout the year, with the addition of a licensed bar and refreshment facilities; the Great Masson and Great Rutland Caverns from Easter until September. A new hotel built at Matlock Bath on the site of a thermal spring has a 'Lamp and Seam' restaurant based on local mining and its equipment. Riber Castle wildlife park, open daily, offers Britain's largest collection of European species.

Day and residential visitors to Matlock can find great variety of refreshment and accommodation facilities—from riverside tea-garden and fish-and-chip buffet to 'medieval' steak bar, from caravan-park or B and B cottage to Trust House hotel standard. Matlock has set its sights on providing for every type of visitor, with recreational attractions such as a lido, river boating, miniature golf and pleasure gardens in support of its landscape's grandeur and surprise. For those with historical interests, Cromford's original fortress-like eighteenth-century mills, Crich's tramway museum, Tudor Hardwick Hall (2 miles south of the M1 at access point 29) suggests the available range—after one has exhausted the dales and their villages, the associations with Izaak Walton, Florence Nightingale and George Eliot.

Moffat, Dumfriesshire, whose waters 'almost as nasty and efficacious as those of Harrogate' first attracted visitors in the mid-eighteenth century, is the most accessible of Scottish inland resorts from the other side of the border. Situated at the meeting of the Annan and Birnock waters, at the foot of Gallow Hill, it is also sheltered, surrounded by fine varied scenery and spaciously laid out. Its High Street, with thorough-fares on either side of a double row of lime trees (with free parking for cars), its crescent (beyond Old Well Road) and the gardened villas which augment the hotel accommodation, faintly recall Cheltenham or 'an exceedingly Scotch and respectable Baden-Baden' (William Black). Health-seekers have been followed by holiday-makers to a centre equally favourable for the hill-walker, golfer, angler or motorist —whose patron saint manqué, J. L. MacAdam, is buried here.

The chalybeate spring was first discovered in 1633, but it was the sulphurous wells, north of the town, which brought in sufferers from rheumatism and liver disorders and made Moffat a fashionable spa. James Macpherson ('Ossian') stayed at Moffat House, now Hotel, in 1759 while working on his controversial Gaelic poems. Burns is credited with inscribing a verse on the window of the Black Bull Hotel. The baths house was built in 1827: the Pump Room resembled 'an educational institution painted white'; the hydro, built near the end of the century, burned down in 1921. As befits its tradition there are fine buildings in Moffat's High Street, including an Adam house, and an impressive solidity about the banks, court house, clerk's office and town steeple.

This clean and attractive little town, with its symbolic fountain at one end, over which stands a black-faced ram to indicate the importance of sheep-farming here, is also a good centre for 'hill-and-dell' excursions —to Saddle Yoke, White Comb, Black Crag, Grey Mare's Tail (waterfall), Loche Skene, The Devil's Beef Tub, etc. Of especial interest to the botanist and naturalist will be the local ferns and alpines and the chance to see peregrine, merlin, kestrel, goosander and oyster-catcher in their native or adopted haunts. Gala week, in August, celebrates the business interest of this countryside, with the installation first of a Moffat shepherd and his lass, dressed in costumes of the 'Ettrick Shepherd' period (James Hogg, 1770–1835), woven by local handloom weavers.

Ripon, Yorkshire, a small cathedral city, once a leading industrial town (woollens), once a 'spa-let', possessor of one of the largest open market places in the north, is of interest for itself as well as for its advantageous situation midway between the Yorkshire dales and the Yorkshire moors. Standing at the confluence of the rivers Ure, Skell and Laver, it makes an excellent centre for exploring the cream of the dales, Wharfedale, Nidderdale, Wensleydale (Yoredale) and Swaledale. The North Yorkshire moors, a National Park with forests, narrow 'secret' valleys and special trails, are equally accessible, as are the pleasant places at the edge of the Howardian Hills, Ampleforth, Coxwold, Kilburn, Byland Abbey. Fountains Abbey, queen of monastic ruins in Britain, is barely five miles away.

Ripon cathedral, rebuilt in the twelfth century, after its Saxon founding, by Archbishop Roger of York, is particularly interesting: it contains examples of Saxon, Norman, Transitional, Early English, Decorated and Perpendicular architectural styles. The two bays, to right and left of the nave, are Archbishop Roger's: into his Transitional walls Archbishop de Gray introduced Early English arches (thirteenth century) and also built the western front; the soaring arches of the Perpendicular nave (fifteenth century) are as fine as anything of the period. There are both Saxon and Norman crypts, a Norman apse, three Transitional bays on the north of the choir, three eastern bays of the Decorated period and fine fifteenth-century choir stalls by a local guild of carvers. The splendid east front recalls that of Lincoln.

After the cathedral the market square is the focus of interest—and a bright, lively scene on any fine Saturday in summer. Its central obelisk, 90 feet high, surmounted by the city badge—a horn garlanded —was set up in 1781. The town hall on the south side, built to a design of Wyatt (1801), was formerly the Marquess of Ripon's city house. On the south-west corner a half-timbered fourteenth-century building (restored) was the residence of the Wakeman and later of the Mayor. At 9 o'clock each night at each corner of the obelisk the City Horn-blower sounds the horn, which formerly marked the 'setting of the watch' and announced that the city was in the Wakeman's care for the night—as has been done for over 1,000 years without break. But, as the inscription on the town hall pediment runs, EXCEPT YE LORD KEEP YE CITYE YE WAKEMAN WAKETH IN VAIN.

In comparison the city's spa days are recent and perhaps less note-worthy: but the Spa Hotel (opened 1909), Spa Gardens, Spa Baths and Pump Room keep this tradition in mind. The first race meeting at Ripon was held in 1713 and to the racegoer the course on the city's south-east boundary remains a popular and attractive venue.

Strathpeffer Spa, Ross and Cromarty, with waters like those of Moffat or Harrogate, came into high fashion somewhat later than either. Although its sulphur springs had attracted more than local attention by the end of the eighteenth century and led to the erection of a Pump Room in 1819 over the 'Strong Well', the spa's first phase of fashion was late Victorian and Edwardian. More extended buildings for both wells and baths were built in the sixties, another Pump Room in 1909 and a Pavilion. Up to World War I it held its own, until change of fashion and the appeal of continental resorts at scarcely greater distance lost it popularity.

The second fashionable phase may now be at hand. Ease of travel and improvement of Highland roads have largely removed disadvantages of distance—a holiday spent away from conventional centres is no longer the monopoly of the wealthy—and the spa itself has been restored, modernised and enlarged. Place has been found for new amenities in an old Highland background—a new ballroom floor, for example, in the Spa Pavilion, a new restaurant, cocktail and sun lounges, golf, bowls and tennis facilities. What was described, fifty years ago, as 'a prettily situated village of modern creation in the centre of some of the finest scenery in the Highlands', is now setting itself out, on quite a new scale and standard, as the focal point of tourist Scotland.

It remains a health resort, with a careful regimen, especially for those afflicted with the modern digestive and nervous disorders, but it is also a holiday resort, easily reached via Inverness airport and offering as much sun in early summer and an hour and a half more daylight in midsummer than places in the extreme south of England. The climate is such that here too sub-tropical plants and shrubs grow freely in the open. In 1898 one of the leading hotels offered as up-to-date inducement 'a cycle court with professional attendants'; now there is crazy golf in the Spa Gardens and Highland Cabaret in the Pavilion. The Pump Room remains an interesting period piece with its original (reconditioned) Edwardian wicker furniture.

Archaeological and historical subjects abound in the surrounding neighbourhood: stone circles, Celtic stones, prehistoric chambered cairns, lake dwellings and crannogs, and the unique fort on the summit of Knockfarrel, formed of large stone blocks fused together by fire. Of the castles Castle Leod, Balconie Castle, Foulis and Dunrobin are survivals among many more ruins. The local ben, Ben Wyvis (3,429ft), on the estate of the Duchess of Sutherland (owner of Dunrobin) should be climbed for the magnificent panorama of the whole mountain and loch environs extending to Lewis in the far Hebrides. A snowball from the corries, to be presented to the Crown on demand any day of the year, is said to be a condition of its retention.

Tunbridge Wells, Kent, is a royal borough with a royal ancestry, and the Pantiles, paved at the instance of Queen Anne, contains one of the three or four best-known parades in the country. Soon after the chalybeate springs were first discovered in 1606 royalty started to come to take the waters: Queen Henrietta Maria, Charles II, Queen Catherine, James II—and they have continued to come ever since. From 1735 Beau Nash ran the social life of the town for many years.

The town is relatively new, with nothing medieval or Tudor in it. Its oldest church, dedicated to Charles I, was completed in 1696, but its best secular buildings are Georgian and early Victorian. James and Decimus Burton were the architects of Calverley Park and Calverley Crescent (1829) to the east of Mount Pleasant, and of other houses; Mount Zion and Cumberland Walk also have attractive buildings of this period. The Pump Room is now demolished, while the former assembly rooms on the Lower Walk have undergone more than one demotion in usage. One can still, however, take a glass of well water on the Pantiles.

The finest natural curiosities at Tunbridge Wells are the strangely weathered Wellington Rocks on the Common, Toad Rock at Rusthall and the High Rocks, two miles distant, headquarters of the Sandstone Climbing Club of Great Britain. Bowles Rocks, Eridge and Harrison Rocks, Groombridge are only a little farther off. James II visited the High Rocks as Duke of York, and when Silas Neville went to see them in 1768 they were already celebrated. With its 250 acres of common, several small parks, recreation grounds and wide tree-lined thoroughfares the town feels as 'open' as Harrogate—and, like Harrogate, it offers much to cricket lovers as well as to those interested in antiques, antiquarian books and new fashions.

For the walker, Eridge, Fordcombe, Pembury, Penshurst, Speldhurst are all attractive and readily accessible, often through fine woodland. For the motorist Castle Ightham's moated manor, Chiddingstone Castle, Hever Castle, Palladian Mereworth, 'Bateman's'—Kipling's former home at Burwash—the National Pinetum near Goudhurst,

Knole Park and Chartwell, near Westerham—Churchill's old residence—are all within easy reach. The historic riches of the south country and of the 'Garden of England' lie all around Tunbridge Wells.

Windermere and Bowness-on-Windermere, Westmorland, two townships spreading into each other without any obvious boundary distinctions, probably have more cafes, craft shops, and souvenir galleries than Ambleside and Grasmere put together, and at the season's height all are overflowing. Still more are being opened, for this is the easiest of access and most popular part of Lakeland, by road, rail or water.

Bowness, the more ancient place, with 'a labyrinth of small streets' as its nucleus, is dominated on the lakeside by its boat-landings and its hotels, some with amusing nineteenth-century touches amid their luxurious modernisation—a stuffed stag's head over the entry, or a photograph of the banquet provided for the Kaiser in 1895 on the staircase. One preserves the Adam ceiling of its pre-hotel status, in the cocktail lounge. The church, Windermere Parish Church, centrally situated, dates from the fifteenth century, its yews from several centuries earlier. Its east window, taken from Cartmel in Furness and restored, is of great age and beauty. The Crucifixion has been regarded as one of the finest examples of glass painting extant. Close by there is a seventeenth-century cottage of traditional Lakeland style.

At the junction of the roads linking Windermere station to Bowness, a clock-tower monument with a new Westmorland slate face stands in tribute to M. J. B. Baddeley, the Victorian guide-book compiler, whose volume on the English lakes was once in every knapsack.

Windermere, entirely modern by comparison, has a situation some three hundred feet above lake-level, so that one of its hotel terraces commands an extensive view of the lake. Even better views are obtainable from the hill above the Hydro, Biscay How, and from the terrace in front of St Anne's Girls' School. The school's premises include 'Elleray', formerly the home of 'Christopher North'. But the best views of all entail a twenty-minute walk, by a lane starting close to the railway station, up to Orrest Head (650ft), from which most parts of the lake and the north-western mountains can be identified.

This is Windermere's three-star attraction—though it has a golf course. In the town itself there are no sights, but one can identify period buildings, both of earliest and secondary development stages, such as a roadside villa of the seventies. Within three miles, however, the village of Troutbeck contains in 'Townend' a fine old Lakeland yeoman's house (*c* 1623), appropriately furnished and open to view, and also the Mortal Man Inn, once meeting place of Wordsworth, Coleridge, Southey and De Quincey. The whole village is rewarding.

Woodhall Spa, Lincolnshire, is a collector's piece, an afforested island lost to view among fens—though with the wolds not far off—waiting to surprise. A sign close to the Broadway points across a grass-grown single-line rail-track, TO THE TEA HOUSE IN THE WOODS, TO THE RHEU-MATISM CLINIC, TO THE KINEMA. The latter, which celebrates its fiftieth anniversary this year (1972), has its own generator—so that it is not affected by electric power cuts, employs back projection—so avoiding flicker on the screen and light rays in the hall, and has only one price of admission—so that patrons can sit where they choose. It is the only film entertainment for many miles around and it also is hidden in the woods.

The town is small, twentieth-century and simply built, with open country round the corner of every road. The Broadway contains most of its shops: from the centre a five-minute walk with 'no tiresome gradients, no noisy traffic' takes one either to the Spa Baths, Kinema, golf course or park. There are four residential hotels, one with the stately ambience of a former millionaire's house and vast park, a control on the type of house being built (local opinion says 'vying with Harrogate'), a prep. school for boys: no other accommodation. Of the two Victorian churches, small St Andrew's with hammer-beam roof to the nave, and spacious St Peter's, with lofty nave arcade of brick arches on stone pillars and oak-panelled walls (Hodgson Fowler, 1893), the latter sees regular use. The Wellington monument, $1\frac{1}{2}$ miles north-east on the road to Horncastle, an obelisk with a bust of the victor, stands by a wood from acorns sown immediately after the battle of Waterloo, showing clearly the rate at which oaks grow. The trees flanking Coronation Road include fine specimens of *Sequoia welling-*

tonia—Sequoia gigantea seldom seen in England. The woodland in and around the spa offers unusual rewards to bird-watchers.

Those who relish unexpected oases may find in Woodhall Spa more than at first appears: excellent golf, seasonal horse gymkhanas, sports championship meetings in Jubilee Park; a convenient base for a spring visit to the Lincolnshire bulb fields or a summer one to Tennyson country; and, above all, the now almost-forgotten savour of leisurely 'taking the waters', while the sun filters redly-gold through the tall pinewoods.

SELECT BIBLIOGRAPHY

DIARIES, JOURNALS, LETTERS AND MEMOIRS

Boswell, James. *London Journal, 1762–3*, ed Frederick A. Pottle (1950)

Burney, Fanny. *Diary and Letters, 1778–1840* (1842–8)

Evelyn, John. *Diary, 1620–1706* (1818)

Fiennes, Celia. *Journeys, 1685–1703*, ed Christopher Morris (1947)

Gray, Thomas. *Letters*, ed Mrs Paget Toynbee (1915)

Hamilton, Anthony, *Mémoires de la Vie du Comte de Gramont* (1713), ed (in French) by Horace Walpole, trans into English by Abel Boyer (1714), rev and annot by Sir W. Scott (1811)

Kilvert, Francis. *Selections from the Diary of the Rev Francis Kilvert, 1870–9*, ed William Plomer, 3 vols (1938–40; new ed repr 1961)

Moore, Thomas. *Memoirs, Journal and Correspondence, 1818–41* (1853–6) *Journal*, ed Peter Quennell, (rev ed 1964)

Neville, Silas. *Diary, 1767–88*, ed Basil Cozens–Hardy (1950)

Pepys, Samuel. *Diary, 1659–65* (1825; 1893–6)

Torrington, Viscount (Hon John Byng). *Journals, 1780–94*, ed C. Bruyn Andrews (1934–8)

Walpole, Horace. *Letters: 1732–97* (1820; 1903–5)

Wesley, John. *Journal* (1909–11)

Woodforde, James. *Diaries, 1758–1802*: *The Diary of a Country Parson*, ed John Beresford (1924–31)

Wordsworth, Dorothy. *Grasmere Journal, 1800–3*, ed W. Knight (1896; 1904)

Yonge, James. *Journal, 1647–1721*, ed F. N. L. Poynter (1963)

NOVELS AND PLAYS

Austen, Jane. *Northanger Abbey* (1818)

Black, William. *The Strange Adventures of a Phaeton* (1874)

Borrow, George. *Wild Wales* (1862)

Colette. *Claudine and Annie* (1903)

Dickens, Charles. *The Pickwick Papers* (1836–7)
    Mr Nightingale's Diary (with Mark Lemon) (1850)

Fielding, Henry. *The History of Tom Jones, A Foundling* (1749)

Shadwell, Thomas. *Epsom Wells* (1672)

Sheridan, Richard Brinsley. *The Rivals* (1775)

Smollett, Tobias. *Humphrey Clinker* (1771)

Thackeray, William Makepeace. *Henry Esmond, Esquire, The History of* (1852)
    The Virginians (1857–9)

MISCELLANEA

Anon. *A Lady's Tour round Monte Rosa, with Visits to the Italian Valleys: In a Series of Excursions in the Years 1850–56–58* (1859)

Anon. *Bubbles from the Brunnen of Nassau* (7th ed 1866)

Combe, William. *The Tour of Dr Syntax in Search of the Picturesque* (7th ed 1817)

Gilpin, William. *Observations on the Mountains and Lakes of Cumberland and Westmorland* (1786)

Gully, James Manby. *The Water Cure in Chronic Disease* (1846)

Harrogate Medical Society. *A Brief Account of the Nature of Spa Treatment* (nd)

Lonsdale Magazine (1820–2)

Pennant, Thomas. *Tours* (1771–5)

Roger, Charles. *A Week at Bridge of Allan* (1856)

Thomson, R. Wodrow. *Ben Rhydding, The Asclepion of England* (1863)

Thomson, Spencer. *Health Resorts of Britain: And How to Profit by Them* (1860)

Wordsworth, William. *A Guide through the District of the Lakes* (1822)

SECONDARY SOURCES

Anon. *Historic Buxton and Its Spa Era* (1970)

   A Pictorial and Descriptive Guide to Llandrindod Wells, Llangammarch Wells, Llanwrtyd Wells etc (2nd ed 1911)

Baddeley, M. J. B. and Ward, C. S. *North Wales* (nd)

Barton, Margaret. *Tunbridge Wells* (1937)

Betjeman, John. *First and Last Loves* (1952)

Bouch, C. M. K. and Jones, G. P. *The Lake Counties 1500–1830* (1961)

British Medical Association. *The Book of Bath* (1925)

Clarke, H. G. *Royal Leamington Spa: A Century's Growth and Development* (1966)

Clunn, Harold. *The Face of the Home Counties* (1960)

Condry, William, *Exploring Wales* (1970)

Connely, W. *Beau Nash, Monarch of Bath and Tunbridge Wells* (1955)

Haythornthwaite, William. *Harrogate Story* (1954)

Hodge, Edmund W. *Enjoying the Lakes* (1957)

Home, Gordon. *Through East Anglia* (1925)

Jennings, Bernard (ed). *A History of Harrogate and Knaresborough* (1970)

Little, Bryan. *Bath Portrait* (1961)

Nicholson, Norman. *The Lakers* (1955)

Pakenham, Simona. *Cheltenham: A Biography* (1971)

Shuttleworth's Guide-book to Ilkley and the Neighbourhood (1883)

Smith, R. A. L. *Bath* (1944)

Waite, Vincent. *Malvern Country* (1968)

Walter, Rev J. C. *Records of Woodhall Spa* (1904)

INDEX

Abergavenny, 136, 154–5
Adam Bede, 48
Adelaide, Queen, 127
Aide, Hamilton, 140
Aix-les-Bains, 78
Akeman, 18
Akemanceaster, 18
Albert, Prince, 27, 151
Aldborough, 18, 80
Alderson, Dr, 109
Alford, 98
Alice in Wonderland, 142
Allan, Bridge of, 155–6
Allen, Ralph, 30, 31, 40, 152, 153
Allingham, William, 140
Allom, Thomas, 108, 109
Alston, 49
Ambleside, 121, 122, 127, 128, 132, 134, 149
Anne, Queen, 24, 29, 44, 180
Aquae Arnemetiae, 17; Aureliae, 17; Mattiacorum, 17; Sulis, 17, 18, 113, 151
Architects:
    Adam, Robert, 32, 47, 152
    Atwood, Thomas, 32
    Baldwin, Thomas, 32, 152
    Billings, T., 68
    Brodrick, Cuthbert, 83
    Burton, Decimus, 26, 180
    Burton, James, 26, 180
    Cann, R. A., 107
    Carr, John, 45, 49, 157
    Deykes, John, 53
    Deykes, Samuel, 53
    Forbes, John, 68, 158
    Fowler, Hodgson, 105, 182
    Jearrad, C. and R. W., 68, 158

    Jones, Inigo, 31, 45
    Lightoler, Thomas, 32
    Palmer, John, 35, 152
    Papworth, J. B., 67, 158
    Scott, Gilbert, 132
    Shaw, Norman, 84, 167
    Smith, C. S., 60
    Soane, Sir John, 68
    Strutt, Isaac, 75
    Underwood, G. H., 158
    Wilds, Amon H., 27
    Wood, John (sen), 30, 31, 40, 152
    Wood, John (jun), 32, 152
    Wyatt, James, 178
    Wyatville, Sir J., 43
Ardennes, 28
Argyll, Duke of, 163
Arkwright, Richard, 91, 92
Arnold, Dr, 129
Arnold, Matthew, 129, 150
Ashby-de-la-Zouch, 105
Ashdown Forest, 27
Ashwell, 101
Askern Spa, 111
Aubrey, John, 137
Augusta, Princess, 60
Augustus, Emperor, 19
Austen, Jane, 32, 39, 99, 124
Aylesford, Lord, 59

Baddeley, M. J. B., 149, 181
Bad Ems, 17, 112
Baden-Baden, 17, 78, 112
Badenweiler, 17
Bad Homburg, 78, 112, 118
Bad Neustadt, 80
Bakewell, 44
Ballater, 150–1

Balneological Exhibition, 118
Barnet, 100
Bath, 9, 10, 17, 22, 23, 26, 28–43, 50,
    56, 64, 67, 68, 69, 70, 148, 149, 151–3
Bath and Wells, Bishop of, 22
Bath cake, 10; ring, 40
Beaufort, Lady Margaret, 20
Beaulah Spa, 101
Belper, 92
Beltane, 21
Ben Rhydding Hydro, 81
Bergavenny, Lord, 23
Betjeman, Sir John, 94, 148
Betws-y-coed, 135, 153
Bingley Spaw, 111
Birmingham Regional Hospital Board,
    90
Black, William, 132
Blackmore, Richard, 145
'Boilton Spaw', 111
Bolton Abbey, 84
Borrow, George, 135
Boston Spa, 107
Boswell, James, 10, 48
Bowness-on-Windermere, 126, 127,
    129, 133
Braddon, Elizabeth, 118
Brecon, 154
Bridewell, 21
Bright, Dr T., 73
Brighton, 27, 38, 42
Brill, 102
Bristol Hotwell, 27, 42, 66, 99
Brittain, Vera, 49
Brooke, Rupert, 147
Budleigh Salterton, 65
Builth Wells, 112, 113, 115–16
Burleigh, Lord, 22
Burney, Fanny, 158
Burns, Robert, 177
Butler, E. M., 20
Buxton, 9, 17, 18, 27, 32, 44–50, 57,
    92, 94, 118, 139, 157
Byron, Lord, 48, 68, 151

Camden, 59, 120, 167
Canterbury, 100
Caractacus, 58
Carlsbad, 78
Caroline, Queen, 31
'Carroll, Lewis', 108
Cartmel, 111

Catherine, Queen, 24
Chamberlain, Neville, 78
Charles I, King, 26
Charles II, King, 23, 24, 37, 173
Charlotte, Queen, 67
Chaucer, Geoffrey, 43
Cheltenham, 27, 56, 57, 58, 64–72, 80,
    149, 157–8
Children of the New Forest, 140
Church Stretton, 105
Civic Amenities Act, 157
Claudine and Annie, 78
Clerkenwell, 101
Clifton, 99
Close, Dean, 69
Cœur de Lion, King Richard, 22
Cold Waterers, 55
Coleridge, S. T., 125, 134, 169
Colette, 78
Combe, William, 120
Compleat Angler, The, 48
Conishead Priory, 111, 129
Copgrove Spa, 108
Corbett, John, 90
'Corvo, Baron', 20
Cox, David, 135
Crieff, 159–60
Croft Spa, 97, 107–8
Cromford, 91, 92, 94
Cromwell, Thomas, 45
Cwm Glas National Nature Reserve,
    153
Cyclists' Touring Club, 128

Darwin, Charles, 160
David I, King, 163
Deane, Dr, 73
Defoe, Daniel, 120
Denmark, King of, 23
De Quincey, Thomas, 165, 182
Derwentwater, 122
Devonshire, 5th Duke of, 44, 157
Diana Adnoba, 17
Diary of Francis Kilvert, 115, 137
Dickens, Charles, 27, 41, 55, 65
Dodgson, Rev Charles, 108
Dolgelley, 9, 136, 160–1
Dombey and Son, 61
Dorton Chalybeate, 102
Drinkwater, John, 147
Droitwich, 9, 18, 64, 73, 89–91, 161
Dulverton, 144, 145, 162

Dulwich, 100
Dunblane, 163

Edinburgh, 79
Edward IV, King, 164
Edward VII, King, 28, 78
Edward, Prince Charles, 159, 168
Elgar, Edward, 58
Eliot, George, 176
Elizabeth I, Queen, 22, 152
Elwell, 21
Embasis, 17
Enigma Variations, 58
Ephesus, 32
Epping, 12, 142, 144, 164
Epping Forest, 142, 164
Epsom, 100, 101
Epsom Wells, 100
Epstein, Jacob, 143
Eridge, 23
Evans, Rev Theophilus, 113
Evelyn, John, 31, 35, 50, 99
Exmoor National Park, 145

Farquharson, Col, 150
Fergusson, Dr, 56
Fielding, Henry, 40
Fiennes, Celia, 35, 45, 74, 98, 99, 108
Florence, 31
Forest of Knaresborough, 76
Foster, Birket, 130
Fox, George, 116
Frazer, Sir Alexander, 37
French, Dr John, 74
Fritwell, 21
Frost, Robert, 147

Gainsborough, Lord, 98
Gaul, 18
Gayhurst, 102
Gazetteer, The, 53
Gentlemen's Magazine, The, 116
George I, King, 44
George II, King, 31, 44
George III, King, 66
George IV, King, 101
George VI, King, 28
Gerrards Cross, 101
Gibson, Wilfrid, 147
Gilpin, Rev William, 121, 140
Gilsland Spa, 97, 108
Glastonbury, 22

Gloucester and Cheltenham Rail and Tramway, 67
Goldsmith, Oliver, 36
Graefenburg, 54
Granville, Dr A. Bozzi, 55
Grasmere, 115, 128, 134, 138, 165
'Grasmere Revisited', 12
Gray, Archbishop de, 178
Gray, Thomas, 121
Great Malvern (*see* Malvern)
Great Yorkshire Show, 80
Griffiths, Moses, 74
Grindrod, Dr, 56, 58
Gully, Dr J. M., 54, 56

Hamilton, Lord, 90
Hampstead, 100, 101
Hampstead Heath, 142
Handbook to Croquet, The, 63
Harrington, Sir John, 22
Harris, Frank, 11
Harrogate, 9, 17, 42, 49, 70, 73–80, 91, 97, 108, 113, 118, 149, 166
Hawthorne, Nathaniel, 61
Haydon Bridge, 109
Hemans, Felicia, 130
Henrietta Maria, Queen, 23, 24
Henry II, King, 102
Henry III, King, 161
Henry VIII, King, 164
Hexham, 97, 109
Hitchman, Dr, 62
Hoete Bathum, 18
Hogg, James, 177
Holt, 98
Holyoake, Dr, 59
Holywell (Flint), 20
Holywell Record, 20
Holywell Spa (Furness), 111
Horace (poet), 19
Horder, Lord, 71
Horley Green Spaw, 111
Humphrey Clinker, 48, 136
Huntingdon, Lady, 40
Hygeia (goddess), 110

Ilkley, 11, 18, 73, 80–9, 97, 139, 167
Industrial Revolution, 12, 125
International Eisteddfod, 135, 173
Inverleithen, 167–8
Islington Spa, 25, 26, 101

Jackson, Sir Barry, 58
James I, King, 23, 100
James II, King, 20, 24
James, Henry, 136
Jefferies, Richard, 145
Jephson, Dr Henry, 62, 64, 170
Jerash, 32
Jorden, Edward, 10
Joseph of Arimathea, 20
Journey to Llandrindod Wells, 116
Journal of the Lakes, 121

Kaiser Wilhelm, 181
Keats, John, 101
Kemble, Charles, 137
Kendal, 121, 122, 127
Kenilworth, 64
Keswick, 121, 122, 127, 128, 132, 168–9
Kilburn Wells, 100
Kilkee, 97
Kilvert, Rev Francis, 42
Kipling, Rudyard, 180
Kissingen, 118
Knaresborough, 97, 100, 108
Kreuznach, 107

'Ladies of Llangollen', 135, 172
Lady Audley's Secret, 119
'Lakers', 11
Landor, Walter Savage, 137
Langland, William, 56
Leamington Spa, 9, 59–65, 68, 70, 92, 170
Leeds Regional Hospital Board, 80
Lees-Milne, James, 35
Leighton, Lord, 140
Liddell, Alice, 142
Linton, Mrs Lynn, 114
Liphook, 144
Lisdoonvarna, 97
Little Walsingham, 19
Llandegly, 116
Llandrindod Wells, 11, 70, 112, 116–19, 139, 171–2
Llangammarch, 112, 114
Llangollen, 135, 172–3
Llanwrtyd, 112, 113, 114
Lockheed aircraft factory, 64
London, 32, 38, 39, 42, 50, 79, 97, 102
Lonsdale, Earl of, 109
Lonsdale Magazine, 11, 122
Lorna Doone, 145

Lucca, Bagni di, 78, 99
Luddenden Dean Spa, 111
Luftwaffe, 42
Lyndhurst, 12, 139, 140, 142, 173–4

Macadam, J. L., 176
Macpherson, John ('Ossian'), 177
Madertie, Baron, 160
Manchester, 18, 80
Marryat, Captain, 140
Mary, Queen, 28, 79
Mary, Queen of Scots, 45
Mary of Teck, Princess, 57
Masefield, John, 147
Matlock, 11, 18, 73, 91–5, 175–6
Melksham, 98, 99
Menuhin, Yehudi, 153
Meredith, George, 28
Metropolitan Water Board, 101
Misson, Henri, 25
Moffat, 176–7
Monte Carlo, 78
Montecatini, Bagni di, 78
Moore, George, 109
Moore, Thomas, 41, 68
Morison, Fynes, 120
Mr Nightingale's Diary, 55

Nantwich, 90
Napoleon III, 62
Nash, Richard, 26, 29, 36, 40
National Health Service, 12, 13, 80, 90, 118
National Parks Commission, 134
National Trust, 169
Natural History of Selborne, The, 145
Neville, Silas, 74, 91, 94, 99, 100, 121, 142, 156, 159, 180
New Delhi, 65
Nicholas Nickleby, 65
Nightingale, Florence, 176
North, Baron, 23
'North, Christopher' (*see* Wilson, Prof. J.)
Northanger Abbey, 32, 35, 39
North Yorkshire Moors National Park, 177
Not Without Honour, 49

Oates, Captain, 144
'Old Dido', 143
Old Pretender, 163

Olicana, 18, 81
Oliver, Dr, 36
'Ouida', 78

Pannonich Wells, 150, 151
Pantiles, The, 26, 28
Patterdale, 123
Paxton, Sir Joseph, 47
Peacock, Thomas Love, 136
Peak National Park, 50, 95, 175
Pennant, Thomas, 74, 96, 109, 121, 135, 145
Pepys, Samuel, 35, 100, 120, 142, 147, 164
Persuasion, 42
Peveril of the Peak, 48
Pevsner, Nikolaus, 31, 76, 79
Picturesque Guide to the Lakes, 130
Picturesque Guide to Wales, 136
Pliny, 17
Plombières, 47
Poona, 65
Pope, Alexander, 34
Poussin, 122
Price, Uvedale, 121
Priessnitz, Vincenz, 54, 82
Punch, 18, 129

Radcliffe, Dr, 98
Radio Times, 56
Raleigh, Sir Walter, 147
Ravenna, 161
Rawnsley, Canon, 169
Regent, Prince, 60
Ribchester, 18, 80
Riber Castle, 92, 93, 176
Richard III, King, 153
Ripon, 108, 177-8
Rivals, The, 40
Roger, Archbishop of York, 178
Rogue Herries, 132
Rolfe, Frederick, 20
Rosa, Salvator, 122
Rowlandson, Thomas, 124
Royal Radar Establishment, 58
Royal Windermere Yacht Club, 128
Rufus (*see* William)
Ruskin, John, 48, 52, 132, 135, 160, 169
Russell, Dr Richard, 27

Sadler, Thomas, 101
Sadler's Wells, 101

St Blane, 163
St Briavels, 147
St Columba, 21
St Leonards, 26
Salinae, 18, 89
Scarborough, 42, 96, 97, 99, 100
Scott, Clement, 112
Scott, Sir Walter, 108, 135, 168
Selborne, 144
Shadwell Spa, 101
Shadwell, Thomas, 100
Shap Spa, 109, 139, 148
Shaw, George Bernard, 174
Sheffield Regional Hospital Board, 107
Sherborne, Lord, 67
Siddons, Mrs, 137
Sidmouth, 65
Simla, 65
Slingsby, William, 73
Smedley, John, 92, 111
Smith and Founder Directory, 69
Smith, J. E., 70
Smith, John Raphael, 75
Smollett, Tobias, 38, 74, 97, 99, 100
Southey, Robert, 11, 134, 169, 182
Southport, 93
Spa (Belgium), 23, 112
Spas of England, 55
Spas of Germany, 55
Stanhope, Dr, 73
Stanhope, Lady Hester, 115
Stansfield, Hamer, 82
Sterne, Laurence, 74
Stevenson, R. L., 156
Stoke Prior, 90
Strange Adventures of a Phaeton, The, 132
Strathpeffer Spa, 178-80
Stray, The, 79
Sul Minerva, 17, 151
Sutherland, Duchess of, 179
'Syntax, Dr', 75

Telford, Thomas, 172
Tenbury Wells, 102, 107
Tennyson, Lord, 140, 142, 145
Thackeray, W. M., 27, 136
Tippett, Sir Michael, 153
Tom Jones, 37
Tour in Scotland, 96
Tour in Wales, 135
Tourist Board Magazine, 134

Tour of Dr Syntax in search of the Picturesque, 124
Tour on the Continent, 70
Trade Descriptions Act, 72
Traquair, Lord, 168
Trefriw, 118
Trevelyan, G. M., 12
Tunbridge Ware, 25, 29, 40
Tunbridge Wells, 23–9,¹ 38, 42, 50, 57, 87, 98, 100, 101, 147, 180–1
Tussaud, Madame, 83
Tyrell, Sir Walter, 173

Ullswater, 123
Ullswater Royal Mail, 133

Verbeia (goddess), 18, 81
Vespasian, Emperor, 31
Vichy, 78
Victoria, Princess, 27, 54
Victoria, Queen, 49, 62, 110, 151, 164, 170
Virginians, The, 27
'Vision of Piers Plowman', 56

Wade, General, 30
Wain, Louis, 78
Wall, Dr John, 53, 54, 58, 174
Walpole, Horace, 39, 44
Walpole, Sir Hugh, 132
Walpole, Sir Robert, 44
Walton, Izaak, 176
War:
    Napoleonic, 11, 67, 123
    South African, 163
    World I, 12, 92, 97, 111, 179
    World II, 58, 79
Warr, Earl de la, 173
Warwick, 61
Water Cure in Chronic Disease, The, 54
Waverley, 68
Well-dressing, 49, 94–5
Wellington, Duke of, 28, 67, 158, 182
Wells:
    Canker (Ilkley), 81
    Chalice (Glastonbury), 20

Christ's (Stirling), 21
Holy (Malvern), 19, 50, 53, 174
St Agnes' (Cartmel), 19
St Andrew's (Wells), 98
St Ann's (Buxton), 45, 47; (Glamorgan), 19; (Malvern), 19, 50
St Anthony's (Micheldean), 19
St Bride's (London), 101
St Cuthbert's (Bellingham), 21
St John's (Harrogate), 75
St Madran's (Cornwall), 19
St Mungo's (Harrogate), 108
St Ninian's (Stirling), 21
St Ronan's (Inverleithen), 167
St Rumbold's (Astrop), 98
St Tecla's (Denbigh), 20
St Winefride's (Flint), 20
Tewitt (Harrogate), 73, 75
White (Ilkley), 18
Wesley, John, 41
West, Rev Thomas, 121
West and South Clare Railway, 97
White, Gilbert, 144
Whitehaven, 134
Wiesbaden, 17, 78
Wild Wales, 135
Willersley Castle, 92, 93
Willes, Rev Edward, 61, 62
William (Rufus), King, 22, 139, 173
Wilson, Dr James, 54, 56, 57, 58
Wilson, Harriette, 62
Wilson, Professor John, 130, 181
Winchcombe, 65
Windermere, 11, 121, 126, 127, 128, 132, 181–2
Windsor, Duke of, 78
Woodford Wells, 100
Woodhall Spa, 64, 105, 107, 139, 182–3
Wordsworth, Dorothy, 105
Wordsworth, William, 115, 121, 122, 125, 133, 150, 165, 169
Wuthering Heights, 146, 167
Wyche, Richard de la, 161

Yonge, James, 31, 35
York, 18